JESUS HOUSE

The Call, The Covenant, The Community

The true accounts
of those whose lives were forever changed
by opening a single door.

As told to Lynne Keating

Scriptures taken from the New American Bible, Revised Edition, at USCCB.org
Used with permission from:

Confraternity of Christian Doctrine
3211 Fourth Street Northeast
Washington DC 20017-3098

jesushouseprayerline@gmail.com

Jesus House

"What a great tribute to the power of God flowing into the world through the daring trust, audacious hope and large vision of human beings who simply take the next step with confidence and love. This is an empowering story with an inspiring directional blueprint for all of us!" - Liz Sweeney, Spiritual Director

"Jesus House of Prayer captured my heart the first time I spoke there. Your ministry to those in need of healing and love is committed and strong, and being part of your work is gift to me. Thank you!" - Paula D'Arcy, Author

"Want to see what God can do through us when we let Him? Come read the personal experiences of men and women who allowed Jesus' Vine-life to flow through them and produce much fruit. (John 15:5) Their grace-filled journey together makes a remarkable story!" - Barbara Hosbach, Author

"I only had the pleasure and honor of working at Jesus House one time, and my experience lived up to all the lovely things I had always heard about it over the years. Thanks to you for your years of service to the church of Wilmington - and I look forward to returning in the future. Blessings and Best Wishes!" - Brother Mickey McGrath, Author & Artist

Dedication

"Beloved, you are faithful in all you do for the brothers,
especially for strangers;
they have testified to your love before the church.
Please help them in a way worthy of God
to continue their journey.
Therefore, we ought to support such persons,
so that we may be co-workers in the truth."
3 John 1: 5-6, 8

Introduction

In the year 1974, in America, NBC made a bold move by becoming the first major network to begin "on-the-hour" news twenty four hours a day. Pocket calculators made their debut and gasoline averaged about 55 cents per gallon. The year began with the Watergate scandal and ended with the passing of the Freedom of Information Act. The Sears Tower was completed and named the tallest building in the world. Barbara Walters became the co-host of the Today Show. Silver reached the unheard of price of $3.40 per ounce and gold made history at $126.50 per ounce. The hit series, 'Happy Days' started its eleven year sweep and Peter Benchley wrote "Jaws." Hank Aaron broke Babe Ruth's record by hitting 715 career home runs and Barbara Streisand had the number one hit song: The Way We Were.

Into this whirlwind, God spoke to the hearts of a young married couple, Chris and Angie Malmgren, with four children. The following is an account of what happened next.

Table of Contents

PART ONE: THE CALL

"For I know well the plans I have in mind for you —
plans for your welfare and not for woe,
so as to give you a future of hope."
(Jeremiah 29:11)

In the Beginning

……………………………………….

We, who were here at the beginning,
have come to understand
that we are really only
simple observers of God's work
and find that we
have little, if any,
inside information
on how He plans to carry it out.
Angie

……………………………………….

Chris & Angie

In 1971, having experienced personal conversion several years earlier and a return to active participation in the church, we sensed a call to a more active ministry – but it wasn't clear what direction that would take. We had been involved in supporting the work of Saint Francis Renewal Center and really loved assisting with retreat work. A short time afterwards, however, a series of changes began to take place at the Saint Francis Center. Most of the staff was being transferred and well before anyone could see it coming, the retreat work at the Renewal Center came to an end.

Looking back, we thank God that we were somewhat prepared for the unexpected because of the faith formation we had undergone and we are even more grateful for the beautiful servant of the Lord, Father Tom Hanley, who helped us during this time. It was out of these experiences and this guidance that vision for Jesus House began to emerge.

With few other alternatives, the prayer group that had been meeting in the Saint Francis monastery began to meet in our home. One of the priests who was transferred from the Center suggested that we write a proposal to run their seminary in Staunton, Virginia as an apostolic center. If we were open to it, he said enthusiastically, he would make the presentation to their Provincial. However, when we prayed with our prayer group and our spiritual director, it became apparent that the Lord was calling us to begin something in Delaware.

And so in the spring of 1974, after seeking God's direction through Father Hanley, we put the whole idea into the Lord's hands and asked God for a sign. The very next day Chris received a phone call from a representative of a new and innovative testing program for schools and agreed to meet him for lunch. The rep asked Chris if he would present the program to one of his clients. On a handshake they agreed that Chris would earn 17% of whatever he sold. That afternoon, during the meeting that took place with the new client the decision was made to purchase $759,000 worth of materials. This meant that Chris would walk away with a commission of $132,825! We couldn't ask for much more of a sign than that! After taxes we had $75,000 to place in a non-profit foundation for the Lord's work. But where in the world was this to be? And what in the world was this to look like?

From spring until fall of 1974 we searched far and wide for the perfect place for this new ministry. Through much prayer and consultation, we were fairly certain that the Lord wanted the ministry to take the form of a retreat house in Delaware. And through the Scriptures that emerged during our prayer meetings, we understood that this house was to be a "house of prayer for all peoples" (Isaiah 56:7).

Then on a chilly October evening, without planning it, about 15 people showed up at our front door. None of them had consulted one another. They just showed up, one at a time, each one surprised to see the others. As the group began to gather in our living room we mentioned to them that the very next day we had an appointment to see a property just off of Kirkwood Highway.

By this time we had looked at many properties but never before had a group of people just stopped by on a whim to see how our search was going. We all began to realize that this, perhaps, was no coincidence at all. Perhaps it was a God-incidence! We decided we should pray right then and there. How powerfully God seemed to speak to our hearts that evening. The Scripture that emerged was from the prophet Isaiah, chapter 56, verses 6 and 7. It was all about a house of prayer and about all the provisions God would supply for this house and for all His people in this area.

Several of the people there agreed to go with us to see the property the next day and to pray while we met with the realtor. Almost immediately we knew that this was the place the Lord had in mind. After praying with our group, we made an offer – it was the best we could afford. The owners, however, had a much higher figure in mind. They had just been made an offer for $40,000 more than ours. Our offer was rejected.

It is understandable, I think, that we were not only disappointed but very confused. We had prayed so hard, we had moved so slowly and carefully, we had listened with all our hearts. How could we have been so wrong? But after a bit more prayer we decided that there was nothing more to do but to keep moving forward. We kept on looking at other properties and begging the Lord to guide us so that we would not do anything outside of His will for this ministry. We wanted to be good stewards of the blessings He had already poured out to us.

It was a full 6 months later, on April 3, 1975, that we received a surprise call from the realtor who had shown us the property off Kirkwood Highway. The higher offer on the property, she told us excitedly, had fallen through. She said that she felt sure that if we were to make our offer again, it would be accepted. She was right. The bid was accepted and on June 30, we settled on the property. We were not at all prepared for what happened next.

"Who are these wearing white robes,
and where did they come from?"
...He said to me,
'These are the ones who have
... washed their robes
and made them white in the blood of the Lamb.'
For this reason they stand before God's throne
and worship him day and night in his temple.
The one who sits on the throne will shelter them."
(Revelation 7: 13-15)

From June 30 through July 19, 1995, the date of the very first retreat at Jesus House, literally hundreds of people from groups such as Cursillo, the Charismatic Renewal and the local parishes began to show up on the property. They wanted to help, they told us. The came armed with tools, rakes, shovels and paint brushes. They cleared the yards, planted flowers, painted, scraped and wallpapered. They sanded and re-laid floors, put in bunk beds and purchased materials to outfit the kitchens, baths and bedrooms.

Members of the Saint John the Beloved Prayer Group, led by Jean and Dan Coyle, brought food for the workers every day. Youth groups came and helped the workers by carrying supplies and running errands. When they finished their work they would serenade the workers, all of whom joined in as well! We could not help but wonder, "Was it anything like this when the people of Israel came together to re –build the walls of Jerusalem?"

"Blessed are those who dwell in your house!
They never cease to praise you."
(Psalm 84:5)

There is story after story of the miraculous events which took place during these first few months. These pages document only a small sampling of the events which took place. It seemed as if whenever a problem emerged, a solution would soon follow. If a particular project came to mind, the person with the skills, or the tools, or the equipment would be only a few steps behind. There were also many healings which you will read about within these pages.

During the first year, we lived in the main house and renovated the garage into a conference building which was used for a Montessori school that first year. Although wonderful things were happening, and the Lord seemed to be blessing the retreats and programs we put together, the first year was a very painful year. Several of the people who had been with us from the very beginning had developed a very different view of the mission of Jesus House. They wanted to form a separate Church altogether. But as the

19

prayer group prayed to try to discern God's will it became evident that we were already part of a church. We saw our ministry as a complement to the church. There was a very painful separation which took place. Still, even that event led us to clarify what we believed God was placing on our hearts. The vision of Jesus House was becoming clearer.

And so it came to be that Jesus House became a retreat center. Over the years, this vision grew and expanded in many ways, but it has always remained true to the original mission of Jesus House – to provide a house of prayer for all God's people.

Miracle after miracle allowed us to build our Chapel, two more retreat houses and even a small convent on the grounds. The presence of the Holy Eucharist in the Chapel made a tremendous impact on everyone both locally and throughout the tristate area – and even far beyond that. Though it didn't seem possible to have even more people coming to Jesus House, that's exactly what happened. More and more of the faithful began to gather here.

Money problems, an ever-present adversary in our attempts to remain faithful to God's will, were time and time again overcome as just the right amount of money was made available to us for each stage of growth and expansion. Friends, families, strangers, stragglers, businessmen, construction workers, grant foundations, financial institutions, banks and more - both at home and abroad - all worked together to bring the vision to life.

To this day, we shake our heads in awe when we walk around the property and see the marvelous work of God. It was, and remains, evident to all here at Jesus House that "nothing is impossible for God" (Luke 1:37).

. . . .

"And foreigners who join themselves to the Lord,
to minister to him, to love the name of the Lord,
to become his servants...;
them I will bring to my holy mountain
and make them joyful in my house of prayer;
Their burnt offerings and their sacrifices
will be acceptable on my altar,
For my house shall be called
a house of prayer for all peoples."
(Isaiah 56: 6-7)

21

Chris

I remember, the very first week we opened. We had just purchased the property. At that time the only dwellings on it were the big farm house, an old, detached three-car garage and a small gray bungalow. It seems that almost as soon as we purchased the property, people began to come from all over. They came for prayer meetings or for little retreats and days of reflection. They came just to walk around the grounds and pray. Angie and I were living in the farmhouse with the kids. The funny thing is, when the people came, they wanted to stay. They slept on the floor. They just didn't want to leave. We really had no idea how they even find out about Jesus House. Word seemed to spread on its own throughout Delaware and beyond. Of course, we had a vision of what Jesus House would become, but frankly, we sank every penny we had into just purchasing the ground. We didn't know quite how to get from where we were to what we envisioned. Then one day, a visitor asked us, "What kind of retreat house does not have beds?"

We had been so overwhelmed by the whole move – such a major transition in our lives - that we hadn't really thought through the rest of the plan. We expected to move ahead rather slowly, offering day programs to start. But it seems that God had other plans. People came simply because they wanted to be here. Then, they did not want to leave. We brought this dilemma to our prayer group and we began to pray for beds.

Around that time, entire families started coming to us from the Dover Air Force Base. They had their own chaplain, but they wanted to come here. One of the families suggested that we get bunk beds like they have at the Air Force Base. We talked about it a bit but before we could do anything we received a call from the Chaplain of the Air Force Base. He offered us 19 bunk beds!

After the bunk beds were in, another visitor showed up at Jesus House. He shook his head and said, "God can do better than this!" Then, closing his eyes and lifting his face toward Heaven, he prayed, aloud, "Lord, we need mattresses!" It was a simple prayer but it did the trick. Within days, we received a call from Saint Francis Hospital. The voice on the other end of the phone explained that they were discontinuing their residency program and asked if we could use some mattresses. "Yes," we replied, "We could use about 38." By mid-day the mattresses were delivered to us. Suddenly Jesus House could sleep thirty eight retreatants!

After about eight months, the children and I moved out of the big house and into the little gray bungalow on the property so that the big house could be used solely for retreats.

By the year 1976, it was apparent that even the big house had become too small to accommodate the number people who were coming for meetings and retreats. There was an old three-car garage on the property next to the big house. We kept looking at it, wondering if it might somehow be transformed into a big meeting room. Enter Wrangle Hill Builders. One of the men who had been coming to Jesus House for prayer meetings told Chris that he would be happy to turn the garage into a meeting room. "Just pay me whenever you can," he told Chris. When he found out that the young couple had no money, he told them, "Then don't pay me!"

Before that year was out, the building was completely refurbished. It could accommodate 50 people. It had two bathrooms, two nice storage closets and a sink with running water in the main meeting area. This became not only the place where we held meetings but also the place where we held classes for the children and teens. It affectionately became known as the "School House." Several years later, it would be formally re-named Nazareth House.

Not long after that, I received a phone call from Saint John the Beloved Parish. They asked if Angie and I could come and present a "Life in the Spirit" seminar for their parishioners. Of course, we were happy to do this. Much to my surprise, however, when the Mass was over at the end of the seminar, the priest announced that I would be praying for people immediately afterwards. In the line of those who came for prayer was a nicely dressed man who came forward and introduced himself as a businessman. I invited him to sit down and asked him if he wanted prayer for anything specific.

"I was in a car accident," he said, looking distressed. "I can no longer drive." He hesitated a bit before he continued. "I am too afraid....I need prayers."

And so I prayed for him. When I finished the prayers, I told him gently that God would give him the strength and the courage he needed. I remember seeing his eyes open wide when I said that. He sat up very straight in the chair, turned to look at his wife, and then literally jumped up. "Let's go home," he said to his wife, smiling. "I'm driving!"

The next day a truck pulled up to Jesus House. It had an interesting logo printed on the side: Let Go and Let God Kitchen Products. We went out to meet the driver. It was that man! "Now," he said, "Is there anything YOU need?" I told him we needed appliances.

"I have a client," he said. "He needs to get rid of all his commercial kitchen appliances. Wait just a minute."

Within one phone call, everything was arranged, all of the appliances were being donated to Jesus House. And with that our retreat house kitchen was up and running.

This is the way Jesus House has moved and grown and survived over the past 40 years. A need arises and prayer goes out, tempered with a good amount of hope and trust. And before long, the solution becomes apparent.

<u>Angie</u>

When we first arrived on the property, I remember thinking to myself, "How are we ever going to take care of ten acres?" Most of the grounds were overgrown with trees, tangled vines, lots of poison ivy and sticker bushes. My brother offered to come to help us clear at least part of the property to make it manageable.

People from nearby parishes came and helped. Truckload after truckload of brush and thistle and sticks and branches rumbled down the driveway for several days. Others came and began to work on repairing the old farm house. It was, after all, more than one hundred years old. I often wonder who first built it and if they have any idea of the purpose God ultimately had in mind for it. Were they praying people? Did they have a vision for this house?

At the same time, people from different local parishes came and brought food so that those working on the house and the property could eat. They came every day.

One volunteer was a wiry, happy little woman by the name of Judy Brennan. She was 8 months pregnant and was also struggling with a few health issues. She came to paint Jesus House, she told us, and she brought all of her equipment with her. Without further need to explain herself, she began. Our jaws hit the floor as we

26

watched her climb up and down ladders which were propped up unevenly on staircases. She carried five gallon buckets of paint as if she were lifting a basket of flowers. The more we watched her, the more frantic we became, but when we urged her to reconsider she smiled at us and said in her disarming Southern accent, "Oh, I do this all the time!"

From the very beginning, Jesus House was a community effort. And it seems, even as it does today, that the Lord chooses the community members He has in mind. Over the years, this has remained constant. We, who were here at the beginning, have come to understand that we are really only simple observers of God's work and find that we have little, if any, inside information on how He plans to carry it out.

....

"I had been away from Jesus House for many years,
having relocated with my husband for his work.
But each time I would come back to visit,
as soon as I stepped on the grounds,
I felt as if I was home!"
Sandy

....

Saint Joseph, the Worker

The building of the Chapel on the grounds of Jesus House is an epic all its own. When we first began, with only the big farm house, an old, detached garage and a small bungalow on the property, we decided to use the back dining room area as a chapel. There, we held prayer meetings and, eventually, Mass. But it was becoming painfully obvious that the little space was being quickly outgrown. One of our regular attendees was a lovely young woman who was a teacher at Saint Mark's High School. She came up to me one day and told me that she was planning a trip to Medjugorje with Father Daily. She asked if I wanted her to take any special prayer intentions with her. Immediately I explained to her our hopes of having a chapel.

You see, I had a dream one night in which the Lord showed me the exact plans for a chapel which, I felt certain, He wanted built on the grounds of Jesus House. It would be made completely of wood and would be constructed without nails, using the post and beam method of building, like the old barns in Lancaster County.

When I told my husband, Chris, about the dream, he listened to me attentively but shook his head and told me that this was impossible for us right now. We would need a civil engineer to do the preliminary work for county approval and we would need seed money to begin the project, neither of which we had. We simply could not afford a chapel. All of this I told to the young teacher who thanked me and said that she would come back when she returned from Medjugorje.

"For the vision is a witness for the appointed time,
a testimony to the end; it will not disappoint.
If it delays, wait for it; it will surely come,
it will not be late."
(Habakkuk 2:3)

With prayer, we decided to at least prepare the property for the possibility of a free standing chapel. First of all, the land had to be surveyed. Chris and I had been participating in a Scripture study being held in our Nazareth Center and led by Father Tom Hanley. We were studying the Acts of the Apostles. Over eighty people attended that study group, and in the group was a man named Mike.

One evening, at the close of Mass, Mike came up to Chris and, quite out of the blue, asked, "Is there anything that you need?" Chris asked him what line of work he was in. He was a civil engineer! Simply, and without the slightest hesitation, Chris answered, "I need a survey." On the spot Mike committed himself to getting both the survey and the plans completed and pushed through the county red tape, doing all the preliminary work needed to comply. Still, however, we had no money to build.

Several weeks passed. The young teacher returned from her trip to Medjugorje and came to visit. She told us excitedly that during her trip, she and the priest she was with were ushered into the sacristy of the Church in Medjugorje. The visionaries were there and seemed to be waiting for them. One of them told her that our prayers for the building of the Chapel were being answered. It was just what we needed to hear. We began to pray even harder.

I asked Father Hanley if he thought the Catholic Diocese Foundation would give us a grant. We had taken this to our prayer group and wanted to ask for a $25,000 grant. "Whoa," Father Hanley said, "You won't get that much. They never give more than $5,000, maybe $10,000, and that is to parishes, not to outside groups. If you ask for too much you'll just be turned down." But because we had prayed and asked the Lord, and the figure of $25,000 had come to us, we decided to send in the request for that amount.

We really forgot about our request for a while. More and more people came to Jesus House and more and more of them began to donate. We had a new surge of confidence and started to think seriously about the Chapel. We decided to re-negotiate our mortgage. It was approved. And then, to our surprise, we received a $25,000 check from the diocese. The building of the Chapel had begun!

A builder was recommended to us by the name of Rocinante. Yes, his name was Rocinante – the name of the horse which Don Quixote road in the classic novel, Man of La Mancha. And although finding a builder who would have any expertise in post and beam construction seemed like in impossible dream, we told Rocinante that it was this type of construction which we felt the Lord wanted.

Perhaps we should not have been surprised to learn that he worked with a group of Amish builders who specialized in post and beam. They came and, in no time at all, the entire infrastructure was up. Once they finished that, Rocinante and his builders came and did the finish work.

When we first started construction there was no way that we could have foreseen the dedication date, but we came to realize that there are no coincidences with God. We had decided on the name much earlier in the process to honor both Saint Joseph and Sister Joseph Leo, who's tireless hard work on our behalf pushed the project to completion. It all seemed fitting now. Could Saint Joseph himself have built this Chapel any differently, we wondered, without nails, but with only wooden beams and posts fitted together perfectly? And could there be any other name for the building except, "The Chapel of Saint Joseph, the Worker?"

It seems that God agreed. On the May 1st, 1988, the feast day of Saint Joseph the Worker, the Bishop of Wilmington came and the Chapel of Saint Joseph the Worker was formally dedicated, the ground consecrated, and the Holy Eucharist placed in the new tabernacle.

… … … … … … … … … … ….

"We ourselves were inexperienced
but it was God who provided the experienced people."

Angie

… … … … … … … … … … ….

The Crucifix

The Chapel needed a crucifix. A local priest offered an old crucifix which had been sitting, quite forgotten, in the basement of a church. It was covered in layers of paint and needed a lot of work to bring it back to its original carved wood appearance. Butch Ciabattoni, a good friend to Jesus House, offered to work on it. It took him months of sanding, stripping and washing. Nothing seemed to be working. The paint and the stain would not come out.

Finally, Butch realized he needed to pray and he asked others to join him in prayer that he would be able to complete the project without ruining the cross. After that, the last bits of paint and stain came off and, once finished, it was not only beautiful, but matched exactly with the light, patterned wood in the interior of the chapel. Much later it was discovered that this Cross had been hand carved many, many years ago in Oberammergau, Germany where, every ten years, pilgrims come from all over the world to attend their famed Passion Play. But God was not finished with His interior decoration ideas.

The Portrait

"Behold, I stand at the door and knock.
If anyone hears my voice and opens the door,
I will enter his house and dine with him,
and he with me."
(Revelation 3:20)

In a similar way, the beautiful picture of Jesus which hangs over the doorway in the foyer of our chapel, made its way to Jesus House after having been forgotten many years earlier. Issy Swarter, who has been a faithful community member for many years, tells the story.

Issy

Let me start with the story of the shop owner and the artist. There is an old shop located on Route 13 in New Castle, Delaware which has been in existence for many years, changing hands from time to time, sometimes busy and sometimes vacant. Many years ago, the shop was being used by a man in the metal industry and in the back, he kept a room which he used for spraying paint on the finished products. When it was in use, the door remained closed to contain the fumes and the spatters of paint which would invariably fly around the room as the paint was being sprayed.

One day, a visiting salesman who had wandered into the shop was chatting with the old owner when he suddenly stopped talking and pointed to the interior of the door of the paint room.

"What's that image on your door," he asked.

"What image," the owner replied.

"Well I don't know what it is," the man said and kept pointing at the door.

"Neither do I," the owner answered. "I can't really see an image on it at all."

The two continued chatting and the salesman left. But the vague, almost indistinguishable image on the door caught the attention of the shop owner. He remembered hearing of an old Polish or German immigrant who had just come to the area and who was destitute and looking for work. As it turns out, the man was an artist. The shop owner tracked him down and asked him to come to the shop to discuss the possibility of work. When artist arrived, the shop owner greeted him and took him back to the paint room.

"Tell me what it is you see on that door," he said, pointing to the spattered paint.

After a while, the artist replied, "It is the face of a man, I think."

At that the shop owner made the old artist a proposition. He asked the artist if he would mind painting - right on the door - exactly what he was seeing on the door. The artist agreed and for many months came and painted a little at a time, until the portrait was finished. He was paid for his work and that was that! Years passed; the old shop owner eventually died and the shop changed hands a few more times.

Now, one day not long after the new Chapel had been built, my son was visiting a business associate who had just purchased this old shop. The shop owner told my son that his business was growing and he was in the process of renovating. As my son and the shop owner walked and talked in the midst of dust and piles of splintered wood, little by little they made their way to the old paint room. There in the midst of the rubble the strange old portrait, covered in dust, was leaning wearily against a wall. Sometime over the years someone had taken the old door on which it was painted and cut out the plank on which the portrait alone now remained.

"Is that a painting a Jesus?" my son asked, pointing to the door.

"I think so," the owner replied.

"Well, does it belong to anyone?"

With that the owner began to tell the story of the image made by the little speckles of paint and later brought to life by the immigrant artist. "We are trying to decide where it should go," he finally said.

My son told him about Jesus House and what was happening there and how the Chapel had just been built.

"It's all yours," the owner told him.

My son took the door and brought it to my house. Excitedly we called Angie and Chris who said they would love to see it and met us at the Chapel. The four of us stood looking at the old picture which seemed to smile back at us from its heavy wooden base. Because of its weight we put it down right in the entrance way of the Chapel; it was just too heavy to move around very much. Looking back, I now realize that this was God's perfect plan. There, just above our heads, was a big empty space above the double doors to the Chapel. We found a long ladder and, struggling quite, we managed to get the solid, old wood up to the top. When we did, the picture slipped into place as if had been custom-cut. Not an inch to spare! It was a perfect fit.

Years later it was learned that this particular image of Jesus looks almost exactly like a very early painting of Jesus which is entitled, "Behold, I stand at the door and knock." Yes, it was God's perfect plan. Come to the Chapel sometime and see. It hangs above the double doors to this very day.

The Statue

Carol

Years later when the prayer group from Jesus House visited Oberammergau, Germany, they found a beautiful, hand carved statue of Saint Joseph the Worker made from the same beautiful light-colored wood as the crucifix. It was as exquisite as it was expensive. Everyone in the group pooled their money and purchased the statue, mailing it back to Jesus House. On its arrival, Frank Bradley, another community member, built a special ledge for it. Frank has since moved away but whenever he returns, he comes to Jesus House to pray and to see the statue of Saint Joseph the Worker. Before leaving, he writes down his prayer intentions and tucks them beneath the statue. The next time you visit the Chapel, take a peek! Both of these beautiful hand-carved pieces from Germany remain in our Chapel today.

… … … … … … … … …..

"If such lives were not from God
we would all be ashamed as we observe ourselves
in light of such faith.
But instead we are encouraged, called forward,
and permitted to aspire to a greatness f
ar beyond our human expectations
and perceived limitations."
Frank

… … … … … … … … … … … …..

Angie

Once again we began to feel the pinch and needed more space for accommodations. After exploring for several years, an architect from our parish, Trish England, donated her services and recommended her colleague to do the plans for our next 2 buildings: Bethany and Emmaus Retreat Houses.

By the way, Trish is the architect who designed the Blue Rocks Baseball Stadium in Wilmington. Now we just had to get the money. We raised almost $100,000 over 3 years' time, but the bank still wouldn't re-negotiate our mortgage. Still we decided to move forward with the project, a little at a time.

When a building inspector wanted to deny a permit because of the type of windows we wanted, Trish called him and sent all the supporting data and paper work which he required and, without further delay, the county passed everything and granted us the permits we needed.

Then we discovered that wells which were on the property had to be re-built for water purification. This meant that another one hundred thousand dollars would be needed. After much prayer, we asked for a grant of fifty thousand dollars from the Catholic Diocese Foundation. They told us that they would approve the grant only if would could come up with funds to match it. But we had already asked our friends and benefactors for so much money we felt we could not ask for any more.

We called a board meeting to discuss our situation. It was difficult to remain hopeful in the face of what appeared to be another impossible dream. The letter was read aloud and the members of the board decided that all we could and should do at this time was to pray. One of the members, still a very good friend of Jesus House, began to pray aloud. In his prayer he told the Lord that the board members had done their part over the past 3 years. "Now," he prayed, "Lord, it is time for you to act!" What happened next was a miracle.

The prayer hit a chord deep within my heart. The next day, I made a call to the Laffey-McHugh Foundation, explaining the conditions surrounding the funds we needed. Before the members of the board came together for another meeting, the Laffey-McHugh Foundation sent us a check for $50,000! Excitedly, the Board made a copy of the check and sent it to the Catholic Diocese Foundation Board. Shortly afterwards we received their matching check! Now, we thought, holding our breath, it is time to go to the bank.

God had been busy. A young banker named Bill, who was a graduate of LaSalle University and who knew Jesus House, had been promoted to Vice President. He greeted us warmly, and with the smile never leaving his face, he immediately approved our loan application. No, nothing is impossible with God! But it seems He was far from finished.

Bill Krayer, a Board member, offered his services as our project manager – free of charge! Bill had expertise as a contractor and, with his connections with local builders, a proposal emerged for two new retreat houses. It turned out that Bill's sister went to the same parish as Troy Oliver, the field manager for the Blenheim Construction Company. Bill arranged for Blenheim homes to

40

order the materials we needed so that we could get wholesale prices. He introduced us to Troy, who allowed us to use his company's subcontractors for much of the work. He also wrote up the contracts for them which bound them to price and time restraints. Before long we had a roofer, a framer, a concrete man and a dry wall man, all working on our new cottages.

A gentleman from New Jersey who came to Jesus House for prayer worked for Anderson windows. He made arrangements for us to get the best windows and beautiful, custom made window blinds.

We were granted liberal terms for the payment of the sub-contractors. Things that should have cost us hundreds of thousands ended up costing far, far less. For example, we found that we were able to connect to pre-existing poles and avoided very expensive electrical wiring. The same thing happened for our water lines. When the county would not approve our use of the septic system on the property, we were able to use the county system.

In one summer both buildings went up - "Emmaus House" and "Bethany House." The year was 1996.

It was just a wonderful set of circumstances, people, and timing that came together to prove to everyone involved with Jesus House that "nothing is impossible for God." The members of the board then painted the inside of the buildings, hung blinds and valances, and eventually added on screened-in porches. We are still awed as we walk around the property at times, and see the marvelous work of God.

If there is one word to describe this time in the history of Jesus House it would be "miraculous." God's timing seemed to take over. The right people showed up at the right times, the materials were affordable and available; everything literally fell into place. When an impasse presented itself, prayer groups met and prayed. The material for the siding could not be obtained, prayer went out and the material was delivered the next day. Then, workers from Korea, Mexico and several other countries just showed up and began to work. Bill Krayer put up the entire framework all by himself – manually! A girlfriend of one of the carpenters stained all the wood work.

We could not help recall the Scripture, "Unless the Lord build the house, they labor in vain who build. Unless the Lord guard the city, in vain does the guard keep watch" (Psalm 127:1)!

....

Building the convent many years later was another amazing experience of God's providential love and grace. It was an impossible dream but, as it turned out, it was the will of God. We have learned that we will never be fully skilled in the practice of the tremendous flexibility necessary to complete the vision which the Lord has in mind. Like Jesus House itself, we have discovered that we are a continual work in progress.

And so it went with Jesus House. Whenever the Lord brought a need to our attention, the money and the materials would soon follow – cars, houses, volunteers, and even money. So did the people who were needed - artists, trades people, construction workers and electricians. We often say, looking back over the years, that Jesus House should have gone under years ago, but here we are.

PART TWO:
THE COVENANT

"When you pass through waters, I will be with you;
through rivers, you shall not be swept away.
When you walk through fire, you shall not be burned,
nor will flames consume you.
For I, the Lord, am your God,
the Holy One of Israel, your savior."
(Isaiah 43: 2-3)

Frank

I am not sure where else to begin but in the middle. My wife and I had been involved with Chris and Angie for a while doing small things around the building and the grounds of Jesus House. We loved this work. The work itself wasn't overtly spiritual or religious, and yet, in its essence, it was just that – deeply and profoundly spiritual, religious and prayerful work. It was work of the heart.

I remember one day Chris just sort of strolled over to me, hands in his pockets, and smiling. He wanted to have lunch, he said, and to talk to me about something. Of course, by that time I understood what that meant: take Chris to lunch, pay for it, and get a job! Believe it or not, these moments turned out to be some of the most profoundly demonstrative and inspirational times in my life, not to mention my fondest memories of Jesus House.

This day Chris wanted to talk about building the retreat houses.... I think... It may have been the "let's build a chapel" lunch. It has been a long time - early 1990's. After going over all the numbers informally, scratching out a number of options and considering their meager resources, I finally made Chris try to explain how Jesus House survived at all. I couldn't wrap my head around it. Forget the building effort. How did they exist? I recall likening the entire Jesus House operation to the bumblebee.

I explained to Chris that, aerodynamically, a bumblebee cannot fly. The wings are too small and the muscular system too weak to allow a body mass that size to get off the ground. If it did get off the ground by some miracle, it would immediately crash. Such are the laws of nature – there's no getting around that. Yet the bumble bee flies. By this time, Jesus House was about 15 years old. Like the bumblebee, it had laughed at the laws of nature! It defied the restrictions of physics and aerodynamics – spiritual aerodynamics that is. It moved forward, not according to the laws of nature, but according to the laws of the supernatural. It was easy to see that something "special" was happening. I just couldn't figure out what it was.

Chris and I would laugh from time to time about that lunch and the bumblebee analogy. We laughed as the Chapel was being built. We laughed as the retreat houses went up. We shook our heads and laughed as the grounds and facilities were improved, maintained and improved again.

The "special" part of the Jesus House, I have come to realize, is the unshakable faith of Chris and Angie. Theirs is a courageous faith, an expectant faith, lived in the certainty of God's faithfulness. If such lives were not from God we would all be ashamed as we observe ourselves in light of such faith. But instead we are encouraged, called forward, and permitted to aspire to greatness far beyond our human expectations and perceived limitations.

They just keep pouring themselves out and they keep coming back to give more. And... they never ask for anything in return. As they grow old gracefully - probably should call it "seniorizing with dignity" - I am reminded that for everything there is a season; a time to live and a time to die, a time to pass the torch on to the next generation and a time to sit back and see the harvest from all the seeds that have been sown.

Forty years of faithfulness, forty years of walking across deserts and through raging waters, forty years of seeing and serving Jesus in one another as we move towards the Promised Land. Jesus House has a future and only God knows what it is. Just so, the bumblebee has been around a long time defying logic and the laws of gravity. I trust, in God, that the Jesus House will continue to do likewise.

WWJD

<u>Drew</u>

We came to an understanding that we were to operate out of the popular guideline "What would Jesus do." We did not ask who it was that was coming to pray with us. All were welcome. If someone made inquiries into the Catholic faith, Deacon Joe Conte was there to work with them and prepare them for the Rite of Christian Initiation for Adults. That is not to say that there were not problems. But somehow God always brought the truth to light and we got through. We saw, first hand that the Lord does not always use the strong but instead uses many weak people, many sick people and many who are struggling. But we all have one thing in common. We have said "Yes!"

One beautiful transformation which took place in our history began when we started to receive groups of high school students to Jesus House for their weekend retreats. The grounds were overflowing with young people! Those of us who volunteered to help with their retreats were able to see - up close - the changes that took place in these kids, and also in the adults who came to work with them. The space, the consecrated ground, the stillness and the prayer all gave them the chance they needed to experience God's presence. We could all see it. Hearts were changed. The Spirit was moving in a mighty way. It was not long before word spread to schools from other states and before long, students from all over the northeast were making their way to Jesus House.

When Holy Ghost Prep Boy's School first found out about Jesus House, they called to schedule their annual Kairos retreat. There is always a priest who accompanies the boys and their teachers for this special retreat. On this, their first retreat here at Jesus House, the priest who accompanied the group was sitting on a rocking chair on the front porch of the main house early in the evening of the first night of the retreat. As he sat praying, a beautiful white dove came and sat down on the porch. It stayed there, he told us, for quite a long time. In fact, when the priest retired for the evening, the white dove was still there. He almost forgot about it the next day with the busy schedule for the retreat but when he returned to the porch later in the day, the dove was there, hovering nearby.

Each day of the retreat, every time the priest checked, the dove could be seen on the porch, perched on the back of a chair or on a bordering bush. By now, several of the adults became aware of this unusual presence and would peek outside during their breaks to see if the dove remained. It did. But when the retreat was over, it flew away. And though we sometimes see a white dove or two fly over the property, never again did one come and stay for an entire retreat. But it made sense of course. After all, the group was from Holy Ghost Prep!

Carol

Year after year, the boys of Holy Ghost Prep return to Jesus House several times a year for their Kairos retreats. The dedication of the men and women who lead and mentor these students is inspirational. Before each and every meal, in sun or rain or snow, the boys gather outside the door of the big house and sing "We are the light of world!" One of the boys in the group always carries a very large, life-sized wooden cross with him. They remain on the porch and keep singing until one of the staff members opens the door and invites them in to share the meal. It is a beautiful sign of the Mystical Body of Christ. The Cross symbolizes the Church Suffering, the singing boys symbolize the Church Militant and the Volunteers who open the doors symbolize the Church Triumphant welcoming all into the Wedding Feast of the Lamb.

Angie

Once, many years later, Chris received a phone call from students at Drexel University. These two young men had come to Jesus House with the retreats sponsored by Holy Ghost Prep. Now, as students of business at Drexel, they felt that something was missing in the curriculum. In their opinion, the course lacked the understanding of ethics and morals. They told Chris that they wanted to put a retreat together for their fellow students at Jesus House because it was here that they had first experienced the sacredness and stillness that they needed to quiet their hearts and connect with the Lord, Jesus. They want to pass the tradition on to others and to this day they return to Jesus House for retreats always bringing with them new groups of university students.

Oldies but Goodies

… … … … … … … … …..

"Everyone who comes here
mentions the same phenomenon.
There is a tremendous peace which is felt
the moment a person steps onto the grounds.
It seems like just a little fragment
of God's peace is here.
Of course, we will never know
what each person took away from here
and where the grace has gone
and what the Lord has done with it."
Issy

… … … … … … … … … … … …

Several years ago Chris felt led to begin a ministry to the elderly at the local Manor Care Nursing Home. With Angie and Deacon Joe Conte, he collected tapes of old songs and organized a group to plan a monthly visit to the Nursing Home. They would play the old familiar melodies and the residents sang along. He always came back with such happy stories to share with everyone even though many of the residents were in the very end stages of their lives. Chris – a natural optimist – was a bright light in the midst of their suffering, reminding them that their hope was in the Lord. He was able to do what Saint Francis is often credited as suggesting: "Evangelize! And if necessary, use words." After the singing, Chris would lead the residents in prayer.

From this outreach a new one emerged. A sub prayer group formed who would go to people's homes, when requested, to pray with them. One such request came from a woman whose son was very ill. The illness was fatal and she had accepted that. She wanted prayers for her son because he could not accept his illness and was struggling in a very deep depression. The group came and prayed with the mother and her son.

Over the course of many months the prayer group continued to come when invited. In time, during the prayers, the son would be moved to tears. Then, it was no longer the mother who made the calls requesting prayers; the son would make the call himself. The Holy Spirit was doing a great work within him. All who were present could feel it. The young man soon became filled with what seemed to be an infused peace and faith-filled acceptance of God's plan, is love and His divine mercy. The illness no longer crushed his spirit or depressed him.

"We are afflicted in every way, but not constrained;
perplexed, but not driven to despair;
persecuted, but not abandoned;
struck down, but not destroyed;
always carrying about in the body
the dying of Jesus,
so that the life of Jesus
may also be manifested in our body."
(2 Corinthians 4: 8-10)

The prayer group continued on in this way. They would gather with very little notice to respond to whoever asked for prayer. It continues to this day at Jesus House. So many people are blessed through these prayers.

"He too prays to God
that his diagnosis may be correct
and his treatment bring about a cure."
(Sirach 38:14)

The Healing Masses, which continue to be held once a month, welcome people from all over who bring the sick with them – family members, acquaintances and neighbors. Once two people came who heard about the Mass while waiting at a doctor's office. Others come after seeing an announcement in their parish bulletin or in the Dialog, the diocesan newspaper. The Mass and the prayers always bring comfort. For some, the healings come. For others their sickness would go into an extended remission, and for some, a peace was received which gave them the strength to let go with love - and even joy - and to let God lead them home.

During these Masses the presence of the Holy Spirit is very perceptible. We have learned over the years that it is God Himself who is the healer. We simply pray for His will. We do not tell Him what to do, but instead surrender the person to His mercy. When John Gray, a former Board member first came to our healing Mass he was given six months to live. That was more than five years ago.

We also think of Jane Krayer, who was in a similar situation and is still with us. Jane is Pennsylvania Dutch and, while she does not fully practice full union with Catholic spirituality, she is always grateful for the prayers and her husband, Bill, loves being a part of our healing ministry. To this day, Bill remains an active volunteer, helping to repair and maintain the facilities on the property.

"I was a member of the Saint Mary's healing community for many years," Bill told us, "before joining the Jesus House Ministry. As we pray with people we can see that it brings them to a point of great peace and opens their hearts so that they can be more receptive to what the Lord has in mind for them.

"Once a man came to us who was filled with anger over the fact that he had a stroke had left him partially paralyzed and unable to continue his work and activities. As we prayed with him over time, the anger finally left him, though his disability remained. It is the Lord's peace which we are bringing with our prayers. And that changes everything. Happiness returns, new visions and understanding of the meaning of life here on earth, and the purpose of suffering in God's plan of salvation are discovered. The sense of victimhood diminishes and the sense of victory prevails. Lives are changed and lived out fully, purposefully and, most of all, joyfully. These are the things I will never forget about Jesus House."

Passing on the Flame

Also very precious to me is the legacy which I see Jesus House is building for the world for generations to come. So many young people come here on retreat and so much happens when they are here. I hear them talking excitedly about their new found connection with God, and about what God is doing in their lives. Many times I hear them telling one another that they are coming back to this place. And this actually happens. We frequently hear from college students and young businessmen who, as a result of their experiences at Jesus House, have brought God into their classrooms, fraternities, sororities and work places. Sooner or later we get a call from one or the other. They want to come back and to bring their friends, or prayer groups here on retreat so that they can experience the same joy and peace which is always so present here. Sometimes they call to bring groups in to do volunteer work for a day.   They all say the same thing: "I felt something special when I was here. I wanted to come back and I wanted to bring others with me. This place somehow changed my life."

It gives me great peace, and certainly joy, but also a feeling of great honor to be an observer of God's plan unfolding right before my eyes. The Scriptures describe it perfectly: "This poor one cried out and the Lord heard, and from all his distress he saved him"(Psalm 34:7).

If You Build

Tom

Of course we had no money, but accounting records and books still needed to be kept accurately. So, once again, between the vision and place where we were, there seemed to be only a great chasm. But by that time we came to realize that if the Lord was showing us what must be, then He, himself, would complete the vision.

The bookings began to pour in. Angie soon realized that she could not keep up with everything on her own. Edie Campbell, a member of the prayer group who had been out of work for a year, mentioned that she had received a job offer but quickly felt it was not the right place for her.   Angie shared that she needed a secretary. The first Jesus House secretary, Edie Campbell, was hired. The year was 1996.

....

"My daughter, should I not be seeking
a pleasing home for you?"
(Ruth 3:1)

Angie

The History of Jesus House would be incomplete without the mention of one particularly delightful member of our Prayer Community. Defying an intimidating and mind boggling resume, Sister Joseph Leo de Frank, a sister of Saint Francis, was full of spunk and humor. A deeply spiritual and humble person, generous almost to a fault, of all the people I have come to know, this little nun became for Chris and I one of the most visible images of the face of Christ on earth. One would not guess that she held two doctorates, was a member of the Board of Directors of Saint Francis Hospital here in Wilmington, and Director of their School of Nursing until recruited by Del Tech Community College to start their Nursing Program where she served for a number of years thereafter. No, indeed. No one could of guessed any of this when they first met and spoke with Sister Jo.

Throughout her long and illustrious work history, Sister Jo longed for nothing more than to lead a simple, quiet life in service to God's people. But she was a good and obedient nun. She cheerfully fulfilled every request made of her by her religious community and the encircling medical community of which she was a part. But simple poverty and service to the less fortunate were hallmarks of her religious order, fashioned in the footsteps of Saint Francis of Assisi and these were also the deepest desires of her heart.

Because of Chris' position on the board of St. Patrick's Senior Center, he became increasingly aware of the need for temporary housing for the poor and indigent – something which could fill the gap in the services offered by our retreats and renewal work. Almost every week he would get calls from parishes in the city asking for help with temporary shelter for individuals and families. When Sister Jo caught wind of this, she felt immediately called to be a part of it.

Without hesitation, she petitioned her community for a year of sabbatical to live and work at Jesus House. Reluctantly they gave her a leave of one year, which turned out to be three, to follow her heart. She requested that she be allowed to stay at Jesus House. Her superior gave her several conditions which would have to be met before permission was granted. She must be able to pay her own health insurance; she must have a car and a private residence. As is frequently the case, it seems, we had no money for any of that but we agreed to all three. Crazy? No, just relying on the promises of God which we had come to know through prayer and the unfolding pattern of His providence. Now it was time to ask the prayer community to put it before the Lord. We prayed that He would inspire someone to provide for Sister Jo during the time she was given to be here with us.

> *"We have confidence in God*
> *and receive from him whatever we ask,*
> *because we keep his commandments*
> *and do what pleases Him."*
> *(I John 3:22)*

God was listening. A dear friend heard our need and offered to pay her health insurance.

Next, Chris' cousin, who had just received a miraculous healing after being prayed over by the Charismatic Community in New Mexico, came onto the scene. He had been on disability but after his healing he went to the federal government to tell them he had been healed and he did not need the disability any longer. The officials refused to believe him, telling him that such a healing was impossible and they insisted he kept his benefits, confident that the temporary euphoria would wear off and his symptoms would return. He decided to move back to the East Coast.

He called Chris to ask if we would like to have an almost brand new mobile home that they would be bringing with them. When he heard about Sister Jo, he brought his mobile home onto the property and hooked up the water and electric for her.

Sister Jo had a home. We called it Sister Jo's Hermitage and there she lived, on the grounds of Jesus House, for the next three years. We were almost there; only one more piece of the puzzle had to fit into place.

About a month went by when Father Hanley called Chris.

"I just got off the phone with someone who wishes to remain anonymous," he began. "Guess what he wants to donate to Jesus House?"

"A car," Christ answered, without skipping a beat.

"What? How did." Poor Father Hanley was stammering a bit. He had no idea what was going on here. "How did you know…?"
That was it. Everything fell into place. It was a pattern that was to be repeated over the years. If we kept our eyes focused on the Lord, and did our best to keep to His will, He would provide.
Sister Jo moved in the very next day.

With the permission of her superior, sister remained well beyond her sabbatical year, spending three happy years with us. She came during a time when I had to be attentive to our children. She became Chris' right hand. Several stories stand out.

After a good bit of prayer, Chris decided that there was a need for a men's weekly bible study. He wanted to hold it at 6:30 in the morning so that the men could participate in it and still be at work by 8:00. He wanted breakfast for them as well, so that they could just show up without having to worry about making time to eat. Sister Jo came immediately to the rescue. On the mornings of the bible study, before she left for her own work, Sister Jo would leave her little trailer, make her way over to the big house and cook up a storm! She would even cook for Bill Dougherty, a homeless man who was living upstairs in the big house. She said simply, "I knew he must have been hungry."

We will never forget the day that Sister Jo took a call from a local church who wanted to know if we could take a transient woman in for the night. Immediately Jo agreed, welcomed and fed the woman and showed her to a room for the night. The next morning Sister Jo found a thank you note taped to the door which mentioned that, in gratitude, our guest had washed the kitchen floor. You can't imagine Sister Jo's surprise when she discovered that our guest had used cleanser on the red brick floor which was now covered in white circles. Once she got over the shock, she called us all in. We all laughed until we cried. Sister Jo could find humor in any situation!

Never once did she complain about anything. Each morning she would drive into town to work. Each evening she would come home to her little one room house.

She had the innate ability and courage to move peacefully with the Holy Spirit. She said once, "If you do anything in love, even if you make a mistake, it will be okay with God." She stayed and worked until she was diagnosed with cancer and had to be hospitalized. She is the one who told us that a Chapel must be built on the property. And it was she who found many of the grants and other sources of income to get the project off the ground.

Years later, when Sister Jo was dying from cancer, we received a call. Her order wanted her to return to the Novitiate house where she could receive extra care. We went immediately to help.

As Chris carried her gently down the steps to put her in our car, she said, "Chris, I don't care if St. Christopher was taken off our calendar, you'll always be my Saint Christopher!" A poignant reminder of her feisty spirit!! She will always be in our heart.

The Chapel of Saint Joseph the Worker is dedicated to her memory. There's a plaque near the holy water shell that commemorates that.

… … … … … … … … … ….

"To strengthen our faith it seemed that often,
between the vision and place where we were,
there seemed to only a great chasm."
Tom

… … … … … … … … … …

The Seriously Ill

<u>Carol</u>

From the seeds of the early days, when the prayer groups from
Jesus House would visit the homes of the ill, sprung a new
expression of this outreach: Retreats for the Seriously Ill.
Somewhere around the year 2005 a prayer group member, Chrissy,
was given the news that she had cancer. She went to a retreat in
Virginia and came back so filled with life and hope that we were
all amazed! Kathy Saturday, who was a member of one of our
prayer groups, called Angie to see if Jesus House could sponsor
something like this. After much prayer, the Board decided that we
would look into this possibility.

In September of that year the first retreat for the seriously ill was planned. At that time, Jesus House could only accommodate about 32 people and the slots were quickly filled. Still there were many more who wanted to come. We were able to recruit nurses and other health professionals who assisted us; we recruited men strong enough to push wheelchairs and affectionately called them "The Pushers." They loved it! They ran with the patients in their wheelchairs; they danced with them and swirled them around.

Soon Mark Oliver, a dentist who worked with the Lion's Club, got involved and helped us to find more wheelchairs and more helpers. All of this was volunteer work. And those who volunteered also paid, out of their own pockets, for all the materials, supplies and food which was needed to make these retreats special.

The Retreats always began on a Friday night with Mass, dinner and a talk. Then on Saturday, the Blessed Sacrament would be taken out of the tabernacle so that all day long people could come and pray, and leave and come back, whenever they wished.

This became the backdrop of our Saturday daytime sessions. We brought in speakers who would present programs and share testimonies on the power of prayer and the mercy of God. During these sessions, the atmosphere was simple but not silent or meditative. On Saturday evening, the volunteers would gather and block all the windows in the Nazareth Meeting Center with sheets so that the retreatants, who were being kept busy in the Chapel, could not see what they were doing. The volunteers decorated and set up the room for a special Saturday Night Surprise Party. When the time was right, we would gather the retreatants and bring them to the Nazareth Center, telling them that we had an unscheduled program for them. You can't imagine their surprise when they entered the meeting room and were welcomed by beautiful decorations, delicious food, bands, karaoke singing, sing-alongs, cake and ice cream!

On Sunday afternoon, the retreat ended with the celebration of Mass, to which all the families were invited. It was a beautiful time in everyone's life. The retreats grew so popular that we increased them to twice a year.

"Peter said, "I have neither silver nor gold,
but what I do have I give you."
(Acts 3:6)

We found that those suffering with life-threatening illnesses were overwhelmed by the sense of being alone. They were afraid, not only of death, but also of the pathway to death. For some, the illness was not to end in death but rather presented them with the difficult task of living with on-going, chronic pain and weakness. One such man could not sleep - ever. It was very difficult for him. But he found peace.

One woman told us, "I cannot do anything. I cannot leave the house. All I can do is pray!" Through the prayer and compassion she experienced at these retreats, she found her mission in life.

. . . .

"Strong wind rent the mountains,
and broke in pieces the rocks before the Lord,
but the Lord was not in the wind;
and after the wind an earthquake,
but the Lord was not in the earthquake;
and after the earthquake a fire,
but the Lord was not in the fire;
and after the fire a still small voice..
"What are you doing here, Elijah?"
(I Kings 19: 11-14)

Maura

I came to stay at Jesus House during a time of great personal trial. Prior to that, I accompanied a friend to help out at a couple of retreats at Jesus House – mostly because she talked me in to it. These were the retreats for the seriously ill. It was amazing to me to see how so many people, with nothing personal to gain, would come together to serve those who were so very sick. The joy they brought to those retreatants – well, it is impossible to describe. It was like a little glimpse of Heaven I think.

67

I was married at the time, and working very hard. I sometimes worked to support my husband who was taking classes for his career and I had little time for anything else. Only in looking back, can I now see that God was preparing me for the difficult time which, unknown to me, lay directly ahead of me.

My marriage began to fall apart. I was not prepared for that to happen and it was devastating to me. I did not know what to do or where to turn. I just knew I needed time to think, to wrap my head around what was going on. I called Jesus House. I didn't know anyone there – at least I could not think of any names at the time. I just needed help.

The person on the other end of the phone listened patiently to me and without hesitation told me to come. I could stay in one of the upstairs rooms in the big farm house. I arrived on a Sunday.

This time, when I stepped on to the property, it was very different for me. This time I had nothing to offer anyone else. My palms were uplifted, so to speak, and quite empty. I needed something but had no idea what that was. I remember the great sigh of relief which billowed out from somewhere deep within me when my eyes rested on the Chapel doors.

I sat in the Chapel day after day during my stay. At first I tried to pray but soon gave up. I could only be there. It seems as if being there was enough for God. Soon, it was enough for me too.

I stayed for five days. I'd like to tell you that I experienced trumpets and flashes of light, or that angels came and comforted me or that something earth-shattering happened. But nothing of the sort took place. I did not receive any great revelations or insights; no plans for my future miraculously unfolded before my eyes. I left Jesus house and returned to the earthquake which my life had become. But I was different now. I was at peace with it. I knew – don't ask me how – that God was with me. Though I did not know the way, He did. I trusted that. I came empty handed but I left as a wealthy woman. I had the Lord. That was enough.

……… … … … … … … … … … … .....

"When I first stepped onto the grounds of Jesus House,
it felt as if the entire world was left behind.
My stress, my personal agenda, my concerns took a back seat.
They were all still there but they were not pressing on me.
I was able to clear my head and to listen.
I was able to think without distraction.
It was just what I needed to connect with God.
And now, years later, I still get that same feeling
when I step onto the grounds.
I have been coming here every year since my first retreat.
I am so grateful to have a place like this to come,
whenever I need to reconnect."
Lynn

… … … … … … … … … … … ….

Bill

The Gifts of the Spirit flowed from everyone who came to help. Each one had a gift. Chris had discernment, Angie had a gift of healing. At each retreat a new person would come and would share his or her gift. And when the team planned these retreats we became aware of the fact that whatever we planned was exactly what was needed for those who attended. It was evident to everyone involved that this was way out of our hands. It was the Lord's work. We simply showed up and said, "Yes." We all had our separate gifts, but when we worked together for the good of God's plan, everything came together as one.

When we prayed we typically had no idea of what the person really needed. But God always seemed to inspire our prayers and the person would receive the grace needed to move ahead. The faithfulness of God was overwhelming. So many miracles took place. Perhaps the biggest miracle of all was that those who came with their specific needs received exactly what they needed. And, as I said, we had very little to do with it. God was moving. We simply had to remain available and expectant. Everything else was in His hands.

We have learned over the years that the Lord gives the grace and supplies the materials and the help only for the times and places of His choice. After many years, the registrations began to decline. It was time, we saw, to step back and to pray to see if the Lord was calling us to "something new."

. . . .

"See, I am doing something new!
Now it springs forth, do you not perceive it?
In the wilderness I make a way,
in the wasteland, rivers."
(Isaiah 43:19)

71

In terms of planning, the Prayer Groups always kept the mission of Jesus House covered, praying to know the will of God and courage to move forward with it in mind. At least once a year the Board of Directors met to pray over different parts of the property. Whatever inspirations or impressions came to them during this time of prayer, they brought to a special retreat where they met and prayed to discern the Lord's will for Jesus House in the upcoming year. It was always so compelling to discover that, though their prayers had been separate, almost every one of them received the same Scriptures and insights. Armed with this new assurance, plans for Jesus House would advance as the Spirit led.

Blessed Are the Poor

"When he saw the crowds he went up the mountain,
and after he had sat down, his disciples came to him.
He began to teach them, saying:
'Blessed are the poor in spirit,
for theirs is the kingdom of heaven."
(Matthew 5: 1-3)

The Board of Directors keeps the finances of Jesus House before the Lord in constant prayer, still confident that the Lord will provide only what is needed and only just at the moment it is needed. Jesus House operates just a tiny bit above water - all the time. It is frustrating and sometimes frightening, to say the least. Over time, however, and not without much prayer, peace comes with the surrender to the way He chooses to work. Whatever is needed to conform to His will is given at the time it is needed - nothing more, nothing less; not a day sooner, or a day later.

The Secret of Jesus House

<u>Liz</u>

When my community first sent me to the diocese of Wilmington many years ago, I heard about Jesus House and decided to stop by one afternoon to see it for myself. Angie was there along with a helper and without a moment's hesitation, the two of them showed me around the grounds, explained the mission and focus of Jesus House and invited me to start doing days of retreats here. It was certainly close enough to the convent where I was living, the grounds were perfect for times of reflection and prayer and the Chapel – well, there was something special about the Chapel. It didn't take long for me to take them up on their offer.

Angie and Chris have a sense of ministry which overrides everything else they do. They never ask the money question first. First, they say "yes!" It's an attitude of trust which I have found to be extremely rare. Their faith is so strong and their trust in God so secure that they rarely worry about money or details. It's not that they are not aware of the need for these things, or that they do not address them, but rather that they trust, quite simply, that God will see it through. And that, I believe, is the secret of Jesus House. It works because of complete trust in God who can do all things with very little from us.

I remember one day in particular. I was giving a day of reflection at Jesus House and, towards the end of the retreat, when I was standing outside on the steps of the big farm house. I suddenly had the overwhelming awareness that one day, I would live here. Of course I did not hear this with my ears; it felt more like I suddenly understood that this was God's will for me. I even told Angie about it. And, as she usually does when the Lord puts something on her heart, she said it would be wonderful. We both went away smiling but never really thought about it again – not for another five years.

It was then that I received the news that convent where I was living, on the grounds of Saint Mark's High School, was closing down. I was, for all intents and purposes, homeless. I approached Angie about the possibility of renting a room in the farm house which I could use for my ministry. Her response? An immediate yes.

She went home to talk to Chris about it. Later, all three of us sat down to see what could be arranged. In the course of our conversation, the idea of building a small home came up. Only three weeks later, the board of directors made the decision to do just that! Where else could such a thing happen? Who else would do such a thing? The whole time they all kept saying that they were so blessed to have Kaye and I, but there was never any question in our minds that we were the ones being blessed. They met, they prayed, they felt God was giving them the thumbs up, and that was that!

When the building project was delayed, and the move-in date had to be pushed farther and farther back, I would have normally been upset and anxious if I had not come face to face with something else which I have found to be rather unique here at Jesus House. I saw the tremendous concern in the eyes of Chris and Angie. They were suffering for me. I hadn't expected that. After all, the delay caused them no personal difficulty; they had nothing to lose or gain by meeting the projected date. But there they were, unmistakably, suffering on my behalf. I realized then that God, who is worthy of my faith trust, had put the burden of my happiness and my comfort on other shoulders. He had put it on the shoulders of Chris and Angie and they would not be comforted until I was comforted.

As a religious I suppose I thought that my trust in God – my faith – was pretty strong. But my faith is challenged almost constantly in light of theirs. I will never forget that. Even today, as I talk about, I can feel it still. God is concerned for me. I have seen it in the eyes of another and I live every day now in the light of that memory, with gratitude and awe.

I suppose you could say that it was Sister Jo – the sister for whom the Chapel is named - opened the doors of Jesus House to the religious women of the Church. We simply went through them.

… … … … … … … … … … … … … … … … …..

"There was no agenda
other than to do the will of God."
Drew

… … … … … … … … … … … … … … … …

Kaye

I was all ready to move into the new convent at Jesus House in July as planned. Liz and I had driven through the neighborhood in advance just to look around. I was so excited about the move that I had to fight the urge to roll down my window and introduce myself to everyone I saw.

"Hi! I'm Kaye. I'm your new neighbor!"

My community had given permission and was already making plans for the room that I was to vacate. But day after day, it seemed that there was one delay after another. It rained – no, it deluged – and the foundation could not be poured. Inspections were put on hold, materials were unavailable or on back order. It was one ordeal after another. Every week the prayer teams at Jesus House gathered and begged God for the miracles we needed. Every week a new issue seemed to arise.

It wasn't until March when we were able to move in. But, with the genuine concern and compassion I experienced from Angie, Chris and the prayer teams, the wait became a time of real grace for me. In fact, it was almost effortless in the light of such love. When the day finally came, Chris called Liz and I and said the little home, our new convent, had passed its final inspection. When we finally pulled up in front of the house, I literally jumped out of the car and danced around in the driveway. I have been living there ever since.

I have such fond memories of my time here. Perhaps the most exciting to me is one time in particular, about seven years ago. Angie and I were talking when I happened to mention that I would love to offer an opportunity for some of the homeless women, with whom I worked, to come on retreat at Jesus House so that they could experience a time of rest and peace and might be able to make a real connection with the Lord. We both liked the idea and, as we waved good bye, we promised to keep the thought in prayer to see if we could make it a reality. Only a few weeks later, I got a call from Angie. It seemed that one of her directees felt that God was putting something similar on her heart as well. The three of us decided to meet. Before long we found the financing, the volunteers and the venue to begin offering programs for women in transition: monthly dinners, activities and day retreats. And so it began.

Eventually, through what I consider to be a divine intervention, we were able to offer overnight retreats for these women as well – a wonderful time of prayer, fellowship and rest. Just as we had hoped, these women began to experience the peace and the joy which comes with spending special time alone with God. Many now see themselves as a "Woman" among women – as someone whose life is vital and important. Many have remarked that having the team members treat them as equals has given them a better understanding of the dignity and value of their own lives. Yes, they struggle emotionally, physically and mentally but they are able to find peace in the midst of the struggle. To this day, Angie still leads the group.

So much of what we've been able to accomplish at Sojourners – my primary place of ministry - has only been made possible because I live here on the grounds of Jesus House.

How often people in need seem to find their way to the property! One night I made my way over to the kitchen of the big farm house to drop off a dinner for someone who had come to Jesus House to stay for a few days. I fumbled with the key and finally stepped into the back kitchen area making my way to the refrigerator. I could hear someone coming down the staircase in the front hall and, in a flash, a woman bounded into the kitchen, gave me a huge smile and an even bigger hug.

"Do I know you?" I thought to myself.

Well as it turned out I did know her but I hardly recognized her. She looked so wonderful. She had been homeless and struggling with addictions when I last saw her but she was now on her feet. Her life was turning around. I can't tell you how happy that made me. It's not often when we get to see, face to face, the fruit of our labors. So many have been touched and transformed because of the generosity of spirit and the love which was shown to them at Jesus House.

Recently, I told the people at work about the 40th Anniversary which Jesus House is getting ready to celebrate. They could not wait to jump in to offer their help because of their overwhelming gratitude for all that Jesus House had done for them.

It is true what others have said about Jesus House. The minute you step on the property you feel at peace. It's almost as if the stress, or fear, or confusion that might be your regular companions in life just flee. The presence of God is unmistakable. Perhaps He rests here. Every day I work with the homeless. That is my job, my mission, my service to God's people. Every day there is trauma; everyday there is suffering. Day in and day out. But when my car turns into the driveway, when I step out and see the little convent waiting expectantly against the wildflowers in the nearby woods, when I hear the little birds, invisible in the trees, I am at peace. I am nourished and restored. I can go back to work the next day, ready to meet God where He is - in His people, in the poorest of the poor.

....

Days of Hope

<u>Cindy</u>

I had come to Jesus House for retreats and days of reflection and, through those experiences, came to know members of the prayer groups which met there. Not long afterwards, I began to meet with Angie for spiritual direction. I remember one particular meeting which changed the course of my life most profoundly. I thought that perhaps God had put something on my heart, something He wanted me to do. But it is difficult talking about such things. You never know how something like that might be taken, or misunderstood by another. But, I had decided I would run it past Angie.

"I think that possibly," I began rather tenuously, "The Lord might be asking me to do something to help women..." I stopped to shoot a quick glance at her expression. "Particularly marginalized women like the addicted or the homeless, connect with God..." My voice trailed away a bit because, beyond that, I didn't really have a plan.

Angie's eyes were dancing a bit as she smiled at me. She told me that one of the sisters who was living in the convent at Jesus House had recently expressed a similar desire. This sister was working with homeless and addicted women and wanted to give them opportunities for retreat experiences. It was something these women could never afford on their own. The more Angie spoke, the more the vision began to take shape in my mind. Yes, this was it; this was what the Lord wanted me to do.

After that initial meeting, the project seemed to take on a life of its own. We approached women from the local community, who could support, underwrite and work for such a project. And without further ado, the "Days of Hope" program was born. We began at once to have monthly meetings for the women in transition to connect with one another, to share their stories and to be introduced to other programs which could assist them. We always started with a nice dinner, and included activities and projects designed to enrich their lives both physically and spiritually.

Then, God gave us a miracle. A few of our team members went to hear the author, Paula D'Arcy, speak. As it turned out, she mentioned that she felt a particular calling to help women in difficult situations. After her talk we made our way to the front of the room to speak with her and told her all about our Days of Hope program. Without hesitation she said she would come to give a retreat for these women – not just a one day retreat, but two full days. No charge! To say that we were speechless is an understatement.

Paula kept her promise. And now, years later, she still comes once a year to spend time with women in the Days of Hope program.

I never in all my life expected to be so caught up in the absolute majesty and compassion of our God. I am forever grateful to be a part of His plan for the comfort of His people. I cannot thank Jesus House enough for being the source and center of this amazing ministry.

… … … … … … … … … … … ….

"I can't tell you how important it is for me
to know that I can just show up at Jesus House
whenever I want.
The chapel is always there, always open,
always ready for me."
Johanna

… … … … … … … … … … … … … … …

Healings

Angie

Once, when the main house needed a new roof, Chris' brother, a contractor with a roofing business, came to rescue. He had given the business to his son and told him to take the job for Jesus House and to donate his time because it always led to more customers. His son agreed and began work on our roof.

Half way through the job the worker who was assigned to our project was diagnosed with cancer. When he made this known to Chris, a group quickly gathered to pray for him – and with him. The following week the roofer met with his doctors to discuss a plan of treatment. But, upon a second examination, it was discovered that the cancer was completely gone! There are no coincidences with God! For the "time" he donated to Jesus House, he received, in return, time itself.

This type of healing is not unusual at Jesus House. Take the story of John Greblunas, a good friend of the community. He had just enjoyed a wonderful trip with his wife and other members of the Jesus House community to visit many of the shrines and churches throughout Europe. John remembered being particularly drawn to the corpus on one of the crucifixes he saw. It was highly detailed with the marks of the beatings and mistreatment of Jesus. His prayers during that trip centered on that image of Christ.

Afterwards, when the group returned, they met for one of their regular prayer meetings, eager to share their experiences from the trip. It was at this meeting that John and his wife made a grim announcement. They had just come from a doctor's appointment in which John had been diagnosed with thyroid cancer. Everyone was shocked and very upset by this news but they pulled themselves together and prayed over John, asking for the intercession of St. Peregrine, who is known to be a great intercessor for cancer patients. At his very next doctor's visit, John received the good news that his cancer was completely gone! The doctor, as usual, could offer no explanation except to say that he had been healed.

Then there was Ross, the young son of Angie and Chris who loved to climb the trees on the property. One day he fell out of one of the trees from a very great height. The bone, the doctor told his concerned parents, had been bent – an unusual diagnosis. With a group of their friends, Angie and Chris prayed over their son. Inexplicably, the bone straightened out.

Andrea Duszak, a faithful and generous volunteer at Jesus House for many years, called in one day many years ago to ask for prayers for her daughter who had been diagnosed with a serious eye ailment. The prayer teams at Jesus House prayed for her for months and months. Her daughter made a full recovery and is a very proud and happy graduate of the University of Delaware!

Several years ago, Bill Krayer, the community member who oversaw much of the construction at Jesus House, brought his sister in for prayers. She had been diagnosed with breast cancer. The prayer teams prayed with her during her many months of treatments. She made a full recovery and remains today completely cancer free!

Arlene Kerrigan, who worked at Jesus House many years, asked for prayers for her step-son Michael. He had been diagnosed with a very rare form of abdominal cancer for which there was no cure and no hope. The prayer teams were already praying very hard for Arlene's husband was also very sick and not expected to live long. Arlene brought one simple request: her husband wanted to live long enough to see his children graduate from high school. This request, she thought, should cover both needs.

And so the prayers began. Soon she was introduced to a Christian doctor who located a research hospital in Washington that was making great strides in the form of stomach cancer from which Michael was suffering. The prayers continued, funding was found and Michael went to Washington for treatment.

Miraculously, Michael lived for fourteen more years and was able to graduate from high school, an event which her husband also lived long enough to see. To this day Arlene talks about these events with gratitude, awe and wonder.

Issy

I remember one evening when I was just pulling up in front of the Chapel to park my car so that I could take part in a prayer meeting at Jesus House. I parked my car next to a couple whom I had not seen in years so I jumped out of the car, eager to speak with them. After we exchanged excited greetings and a few hugs, I realized that I had left my keys in the car which was now locked.

My friends and I started to pray. I really could not imagine that the Lord could do much to help me with this situation. But still we prayed, asking the Lord to perhaps help me find an extra set of keys. After we made this request, we stopped praying and I rummaged through my purse, but no car keys. Way in the corner however, I found 2 old keys on a ring. I couldn't imagine why I had them since they were from an old Cadillac – and my car was anything but a Cadillac. "Well, these won't help," I said. But my friend told me to give them a try. Thinking that I had nothing to lose by at least humoring her, I put the key into the lock. It slid in with no trouble. "Hmm," I thought, "that's funny!" I turned the key. The door opened instantly and we all starting praising God. We were amazed.

I was a bit skeptical though. What if this really was my car key and was simply mismarked. I hopped behind the steering wheel and tried the key in the ignition. It did not fit at all! Impossible, I thought! Yet there it was. God had indeed given us a little miracle. Someone once told me that God waits to be asked. On this night, there was no doubt in my mind that God moved simply because we asked.

Chris

During one very hot summer when my friends and I were driving to a prayer meeting in the desert area of New Mexico, a tire blew on my car. We pulled in to a garage and were told that all four tires were separating because of the intense heat. I knew we were in trouble. We were in a very remote part of the desert and the garage did not look like a place that anyone would come for tires or repairs. It was painfully evident that they kept no inventory on hand and consequently, I thought, no tires!

But the garage man smiled at me and shook his head. "You're one lucky guy," he said. "I ordered a set of tires a couple years back and they've been sitting back against a wall in the garage ever since. I ordered them for a man who never came back to get the work done."

He brought us to the back of the garage and sure enough, there they were – four steel belted tires in excellent condition. The garage owner said he was glad to finally get rid of them and charged us only $100.00 for the whole job!

....

There was one little woman who showed up at Jesus House many years back. She just came to pray, silently in front of the Blessed Sacrament. Her name was May. Though we really never spoke much, over the years she taught many of us how to accept everything as from the hand of God. "I am just a little ball in the hands of God," she often said.

May had lived a very difficult life which became even more difficult when she became pregnant in high school. The child had to be given up for adoption. That was quite some time ago when children given up for adoption were taken away from their mothers before they could see or hold their babies. May had never had the chance to know anything about the child, a baby girl. Many, many years later, just a short time before she died, May's daughter managed to find her! Much to May's surprise and delight, her daughter told her that she, too, had a little girl now, and had named her "May."

Drew

I discovered a large growth on my neck. I had already been to the doctor and was scheduled for surgery so that it could be removed. I decided to ask the prayer team at Jesus House to pray over me before the operation. The next day, when I woke up, the growth was gone - completely gone! The poor doctor was afraid that I was going to sue him for a false diagnosis, but I assured him over and over again that it was prayer that caused this to happen. He just couldn't wrap his head around it because he could not explain it in medical terms.

These were the physical miracles. But for me, the most astounding miracles took place in the spiritual realm. Hearts and minds were touched and changed! To me, it was like the water being changed into wine. There were so many of these quiet and quite invisible changes that took place all the time. Yes, we prayed for them even though we hardly knew how to pray or what to ask for. We simply prayed.

....

One day Chris walked into the Chapel and found a man lying on the floor crying. He walked over to the man carefully and put his hand on the man's shoulder. "Can I be of any help," he asked gently.

The man explained that he had been in the state hospital for quite some time. Angie had come to visit him and had prayed with him. She had asked him to consider joining a church community once he was strong enough to be released. He took her advice and had joined a local church community. But this community told him to stop taking the medication which the doctors had prescribed for him and to simply rely on God to heal him. He followed their

89

advice but quickly went downhill. Confused and very depressed he made his way to Jesus House. He had no idea what to do next.

Chris felt rather inadequate in the face of this man's dilemma, but reached for a Bible which was on a nearby book shelf and began to pray over the man as he lay on the floor. Chris opened the bible and read, "Thank God for the herbs of the field. He gave them to his people to be healed." At those words, the man stood up and blinked. It was as if a light went on somewhere deep inside of him. After a brief conversation, he told Chris that he suddenly realized that God was indeed answering his prayers – through the medication prescribed for him! He knew it was necessary to take his medications for God to continue working in his life. He made the commitment to be faithful to his medication and he did it! He remains happy and healthy today and has made it his life's focus to work with troubled kids.

....

"Do you see this woman?
When I entered your house,
you did not give me water for my feet,
but she has bathed them with her tears
and wiped them with her hair."
(Luke 7:44)

Delores

A friend of mine invited me to attend a presentation at Jesus House. Father Hanley was giving a day of reflection. When he spoke I started crying and I could not stop. Once the tears slowed down a bit, I looked up and found that many others in the room – there were about 80 of us – were crying. I didn't really understand why the tears came, but in retrospect, I think it was because I was encountering Truth and I couldn't quite get away from it. You see, Father said that each of us had to forgive someone, and almost immediately I thought of my mother. The experience was very strong. In fact, I had the memory of the smell of the apron she always wore in the kitchen.

As I sat there, playing that old familiar tape in my mind, recounting all the reasons that she should not be forgiven, something inside of me started to change – perhaps, to melt. It seemed to me that was a fire inside of me which I had never felt before. It had been unable to warm me because this fire was encased in ice – a deep, impenetrable prison of ice. Then it came: the desire to change, the desire to experience the burning delight of love. I knew at once that, even though my mother was deceased, I still needed to forgive her. That's where the tears came from. Maybe it was the overflow of all that ice melting away. When the evening was coming to a close, I could hardly stand. The people around me helped me to my feet. That was my first experience at Jesus House; it was about 30 years ago. I have never left.

Over the years I have come for retreats and days of reflection, for meetings and seminars and just to sit in the chapel and be close to the Blessed Sacrament. I continue to volunteer as my time and my health allow. What can I say? This is the place I first fell in love with God. When I come to Jesus House, I experience His love all over again and I have more love to give away when I leave. Because of Jesus House my life has changed and will never, ever be the same.

I have had some very difficult trials over the years, but I am no longer crushed by them. I know I am not alone – spiritually or physically. I have fast and faithful friends whom I have met at Jesus House and they stand by my side to this day, ready once again to help me to my feet. The effect of Jesus House and it's ministries have carried over to my family as well. And my children are friends with the children of my friends. These friendships and connections continue to grow and blossom. Our kids have married the kids of others whom we met at Jesus House - from prayer groups and retreats. I can't help but feel somewhat proud – honored really – that my husband and I have been a part of the work and ministry of Jesus House, all of which works to help raise up a generation of saints!

Mauro

It should be obvious now, if you have read this far, that we who come to Jesus House usually come seeking healing – physical healing, emotional healing, spiritual healing. And the building into which we usually first step foot is the chapel. I like to call it our medicine cabinet. We come there murmuring the Scripture we repeat at Mass, "Lord, I am not worthy...say but the word and my soul shall be healed." We come seeking Jesus, the divine Healer. He does not practice medicine, he creates it! His medicine has only good side effects.

If I live to be one hundred I will never be able to thank Chris and Angie enough for sharing their gift of faith with me, with the world! Their faith makes believers out of us all. They went forward, seeking only the will of God and not knowing the outcome.

They have proven to us all that we are only 12 inches away from Heaven. That is, we are stuck in our own heads, in our own logic, in our own world of never ending information. We have to travel just 12 inches downward and begin to live in our hearts, to trust with our hearts and to love – to love God by loving one another. Here we are, forty years later, still moving forward, still working to glorify God in our thoughts, words and deeds, still calling out, "Thy Kingdom come!"

Rocky Roads

"Do not fear, for I have redeemed you;
I have called you by name: you are mine.
When you pass through waters, I will be with you;
through rivers, you shall not be swept away.
When you walk through fire, you shall not be burned,
nor will flames consume you."
(Isaiah 43: 1 – 2)

<u>Angie</u>

Times have not always been easy. Jesus House had to grow and evolve as any other community would do. There were disagreements as to the direction Jesus House should take and as to the spirituality, mission and vision of the community. With all the inroads for the growth of ecumenism, there came a time when Jesus House had to come to terms with its own identity. What did Jesus want from this community, this call to service, this land?

After many tears, and prayers and meetings, it was at last determined that Jesus House was to remain Catholic, and as such faithful to the Catholic Church. This was a very difficult decision to reach. As a result of this, a great many supporters and community members left to follow a more non-denominational pathway. But in the end, it seemed that the Lord has approved. Jesus House continues on a path of service to all God's people while remaining faithful to the Catholic Church.

There were also many financially difficult times. For example, several years after Jesus House opened, Chris lost his job and the money seemed to dry up quickly. Jesus House was facing the very real possibility of having to close. There was no money for the family to live on, and there was no health insurance.

To make matters worse a notice was received from the IRS. Jesus House was being audited. Chris and I met with our spiritual director, Father Tom Hanley. We were afraid, we told him, that Jesus House would have to be sold. He encouraged us to pray and to persevere. Through Father Hanley's connections, I was offered a job with the Office of Justice and Peace at the Diocese of Wilmington; but certainly this was not enough to help Jesus House. The IRS was sure that Jesus House had not been properly reporting its income and were looking to exact more taxes. We went to see Father Hanley a second time. "Give it one more week," he encouraged us, "and pray!" The prayer teams were working over-time. Then, God moved.

The IRS, upon finishing their investigation, discovered that they owed quite a bit of money to Jesus House. The IRS had been overpaid, not the opposite. With the new money that came in and with the income I was now earning, Jesus House would keep its doors open.

<u>Angie</u>

We knew that we wanted Stations of the Cross that were unique, though we did not know exactly what we wanted. Then, one day, we got a call from Saint Mark's High School. They had a beautiful set of Stations of the Cross which had been donated to them but which had not been used since money for a new set had been donated to them. These unique, hand-made Stations of the Cross had been stored in a basement of the school and the administration now wanted them removed to make room for other projects. Needless to say, we were interested in them. Chris and I went to see them and we knew right away that they were perfect!

These Stations of the Cross, as unique as they are unconventional, are in place today, circling the ground on which our chapel is built.

....

"Now the Lord is the Spirit,
and where the Spirit of the Lord is,
there is freedom."
(2 Corinthians 3: 17)

Drew

Jesus House is a spiritual, Holy Spirit thing. It defies logic and planning. Even those of us who have been on the board of directors have come to realize – the hard way – that the things of the Lord often do not work according to logic and planning.

The Holy Spirit is here at Jesus House. He becomes active at certain times though most of us cannot tell exactly when or where He will begin to disclose His presence to us. The biggest thing is that the moment you drive on to the property, or step on to the property, this tremendous peace settles over you. But beyond that you don't know when the Holy Spirit will come or how He will work at any given moment. It is like that even for those of us who just pass through.

"The wind blows where it wills,
and you can hear the sound it makes,
but you do not know where it comes from
or where it goes;
so it is with everyone who is born of the Spirit."
(John 3:8)

Jesus House has never really been defined with concrete boundaries. Otherwise, how could it live and move and breathe in the Holy Spirit? It took several years before we really caught the vision of a retreat house. We who were part of Jesus House in the beginning just simply showed up. There was no agenda other than to do the will of God. And it has stayed that way over the years. But that is the nature of the Holy Spirit, isn't it?

God uses not only the people, places and things of Jesus House; He uses all of it – even the grounds! I sometimes brought my grandson, Hunter, with me when I came to Jesus House to pray. We would walk around the grounds and sometimes we would find little things that people left – a medal, a little book, or a pebble on a tree stump. People often like to leave a little bit of themselves on this holy ground.

People come because the property is open! It is available to them. And when they step onto the grounds, they can feel the presence of God. In the stillness and solitude of the property they can hear Him speaking to their hearts. His Spirit is always here. His grace is always present. And when they stop to take notice and to listen, the Lord can begin to use them. So many people have said, "I walk in here and I am blessed with the strength I need to be here to do what I need to do." We may never know, in this life, who they are, why they came or where they have gone.

As I see it, the possibility of Jesus House came forward as a result of the Charismatic renewal taking place in the Church. I had heard about it but Chris and Angie were the first people I ever met who seemed willing to put the Gifts of the Holy Spirit into action – or at least to give them a chance – and I needed to see that. I mean, what did it really mean to praise the Lord? What did it mean to speak in tongues? The Lord used their 'yes' to help us become more aware and docile to the movement of the Holy Spirit and it seemed to me, for the first time, that the Catholic Faith was like that treasure chest we hear about in Scripture. The treasures were all in there, but I had never seen them before. Prior to the Renewal we were somewhat discouraged from even reading the Bible for fear of mistakes in understanding it. But, then again, Scripture tells us, "Do not fear; only believe" (Luke 8:50). The whole experience of getting to know the Bible and trying to put virtue into practice was wonderful for me!

Even the name 'Jesus House' did not come in the beginning. We just started calling it Jesus House because His presence is so strong. It was only much later that the name, "Jesus House of Prayer," was considered and even then, it seemed that what God had in mind was something more like a living organism which changed, grew, moved, declined and grew again - much like all of His creatures. It has been said many times that the name keeps us from getting funds in some cases. We talked about it but decided never to change it.

As is often the case with new things, there were many people who misunderstood what Jesus House was about and why it was in existence at all. It was viewed skeptically, even as a cult at times. In the beginning, priests would come to sort of investigate Jesus House, to see what it was all about and to keep an eye on things. Many of them had such amazing experiences here that they decided to stay and help. Little by little, God's plan was unfolding. I guess we just have to get used to the idea that the unfolding will never cease. But as I have said, that seems to be the nature of the Holy Spirit.

<u>Joe</u>

When we were doing all the physical work necessary to get the main house in shape for the first retreat weekend, I worked with other volunteers on whatever project presented itself. Joyce, my wife, would just show up with a pot of goulash for the workers. It was completely unplanned, very much needed and greatly appreciated. I only wish that more people could have experienced what we did. It was obvious that God was with us as we worked. The outpouring of appreciation and gratitude and the unmitigated joy that the workers exhibited was not only very heart-warming but also seemed to me like a little taste of Heaven.

Two Oblates of Saint Francis de Sales who had been teaching in Allentown just showed up one day and said that they would help us to present a retreat. And so they did! Their experience here was so powerful, not only to those who attended but to Father Bob and Father Tony themselves, that when the retreat was all over, they published a book based on the events which took place.

It is safe to say that it was during this time that I first became very aware of the presence and movement of the Holy Spirit in my life. I had become very comfortable with my life of planning and rationality, but at Jesus House it all seemed like so much chaos that at times I felt very helpless. Then, as I stood back and watched, I saw everything come together.

"Jesus took Peter, James, and John his brother,
and led them up a high mountain by themselves.
And he was transfigured before them;
his face shone like the sun
and his clothes became white as light.
And behold, Moses and Elijah appeared to them,
conversing with him.
Then Peter said to Jesus in reply,
"Lord, it is good that we are here."
(Matthew 17: 1- 4)

"It is good to be here!" Those words were proudly placed on the first banner we put up in the big house. I could not help but remember that Jesus admonished Peter when Peter wanted to stay on Mount Tabor rather than go back down the mountain to return to his every-day life. That is what it felt like to those of us who came, and worked and prayed. "It is good to be here!" That is what each of us felt deep within our hearts. I don't remember all their names, but I can see most of their faces. So many people came here – and they each wanted to stay. And so the banner was made and hung in a prominent place for all to see.

One day, when I was in the middle of a big project at Jesus House, I needed a little rest and went down to stand and pray for a while on a little bridge which was built over the stream that runs through the property. I thought that, over time, the water would have moved or dried up, but it never did. As time went on we built little steps down to the water so that people could come and sit and enjoy the unexpected explosion of nature that lay hidden and quiet not far away from the noise and traffic of the nearby highway.

101

On that day, as I stood and looked around, thanking God for this little taste of Heaven, I noticed that the tree branches on the other side of the stream formed a triangle. I thought of the Holy Trinity. All weekend long I held that image in my mind and all weekend long, I meditated on the Trinity.

That was perhaps my first exposure to prayer and nature...the triangle, the water... I began to see the connection which exists so naturally between God and nature, and the way He so often uses nature to help us to know Him better. His parables often center around trees or vines, or a grain of wheat, or even the wind. I remembered that Jesus often appeared to his disciples near water and here He was, once again, making Himself known near a body of water. One day, a very calm day, as I was sitting by the little stream, a very great storm came up from nowhere and I remembered the apostles who were caught off guard in just such a storm at sea.

"Yes," I remember thinking. "It is good for us to be here."

… … … … … … … … … … ……

"It has always been that way at Jesus House.
Once you step onto the property,
you know you are on holy ground."
Joyce

… … … … … … … … … … ….

In early 1975 Father Ralph Martin came to Jesus House and celebrated our first ever Charismatic Mass. We were like gluttons when we were introduced to the Gifts of the Holy Spirit. Certainly we had read about the gifts of the Holy Spirit in Scripture but we never realized that these gifts were available to us. Deep within our souls we had always hoped to see their manifestations within the people of God. These Masses fed our spirits and so it was a joy to attend, to listen, to learn and to experience this new outpouring of the Holy Spirit within the Church. Such experiences are not easily forgotten. Instead they stay with you and continue feeding you long after the experience has ended. It is the memory of these things that helps you to keep moving forward in times of trial or suffering.

As we age, the experiences become more personal and words can no longer fully describe them. It is much like the love of a couple who has grown old together. Words are barely needed. All that is needed is the presence of the other. That is how the Holy Spirit works.

As we ourselves grew in the gifts of the Holy Spirit, so Jesus House grew. Whatever was needed was provided at the time it was needed. I don't suppose this part of Jesus House will ever change.

When any of us began to feel the least bit tired or dry, God sent someone new. When a new pastor was assigned to Resurrection Parish, the former pastor, Father Dan Gerres, came to work with the prayer team and to be one of the presenters for retreats. It went on like that for many years. More and more parishes became aware of Jesus House and more and more people, from all walks of life, found their way onto the grounds.

Deacon Joe Conte comes to mind. His dad had a grocery store in Philadelphia. Deacon Joe had studied for 7 years in the St. Charles Borromeo seminary before he realized he was not called to the priesthood. He married, had children and eventually became a deacon. Still he felt that God had something more for him to do. Fr. Ralph Martin told him to go see Chris Malmgren at Jesus House, and a long and fruitful relationship was forged. Joe remained faithful and true to Jesus House, helping Angie and Chris to plan and present days of reflection and renewal right up until the day of his death not long ago.

Seventy Times Seven

"We know that all things work for good
for those who love God,
who are called according to his purpose."
(Romans 8:28

Lee

Had it not been for the people of the charismatic prayer community, not only in my own parish, but on the diocesan level as well, I would never be able to share the story of God's incredible love and mercy in my life. Many of those who ministered to me and who have prayed for me, helped me and supported me during the most difficult times in my journey of faith, are members of the Jesus House family of prayer warriors.

Just after becoming a Catholic I faced a number of tragedies in my life: My father passed away and my wife was diagnosed with cancer. I praise God that my wife was successfully treated and has remained cancer free for over 40 years. But not long after these two trials, my only brother was killed senselessly by a man in a drunken rage, and my beautiful 16 year old daughter was killed in a separate incident by a drunk driver.

I know that it was only because of the ceaseless support and prayers of the Charismatic Faith Community that I was able to embrace the divine love and mercy of God and the strength to forgive not only each of these people, but God himself, whom, I discovered, has carried me through each and every trial.

Since that time I have been able to minister to hundreds of people from parishes, local prayer groups and even to those in prison and have been blessed to assist over one hundred inmates turn their lives over to the Lord.

....

PART THREE: THE COMMUNITY

Come Apart and Rest Awhile

………………………………….

"If I live to be one hundred,
I will never be able to thank Chris and Angie enough
for sharing their gift of faith with me ,
with the world!
Their faith makes believers out of us all. "
Mauro

………………………………………

Drew

Because of the name we bore, people came. It seemed reminiscent of the days when hundreds gathered around Jesus when He first started his ministry. There were rich men and poor men, there were fishermen, tax collectors, women of independent means and women of ill repute. But whoever came to receive ended up longing to give. They would do whatever was needed. This was, and remains today, quite literally a place where the Spirit of Jesus is present. And we move according to that Spirit.

So many who came through Jesus House really helped me build my faith. I remember a family who came here for a while and then felt called to go to Israel to minster to the Christians living there. The prayer community prayed with them and off they went. They took their entire family and moved to Israel. This is very typical of the things that happen here at Jesus House. If I had to call it something, I'd call it the clearing house, the resting station, for all pilgrims on the journey of faith.

Elaine Donald, who worked tirelessly with the Franciscans, was one such person. She taught Ignatian Contemplative Spirituality and the members of the Jesus House prayer community benefited greatly by her classes, her presence and most of all by her beautiful example. When the whole front yard was weeds and no one could even get to the building she pitched in to help clear the way. When that was finished someone put a paint brush in her hand and she painted the entire front porch! She often described the spiritual journey this way: "The journey of the soul is like a person who is making his way along a trail. When he comes upon another along the way, he stops and asks which might be the best way to follow along the trail. And that person points the way."

....

Till There Was You

"Nations shall behold your vindication,
and all kings your glory;
You shall be called by a new name
bestowed by the mouth of the Lord."
(Isaiah 62:2)

<u>Johanna</u>

I am a newbie – both to Jesus House and to the Catholic faith. So it is delightful for me to hear the old stories. It's amazing how much my own experience at Jesus House is so similar to many of these accounts. I, too, felt such a power, such a peace when I would wander into the little dining room in the main house, only to learn that the space had once been used as the chapel where Mass was celebrated and the bread and wine was changed into the body and blood of Christ.

"Well, of course I would feel something," I said to myself, laughing!

It was late in my life when I was first introduced the spirituality of Padre Pio – now a saint in the Catholic Church. It was his life which inspired me to become Catholic. When I first stepped foot in a Church I ended up sitting next to Angie. A coincidence? I don't think so! Of course I now realize this was all God's plan for me though I didn't know it at the time. She invited me to the faith sharing group at Jesus House.

"Fantastic," I said in reply, "Just what I need!"

At those meetings I met other wonderful, faith-filled people and soon began to attend the Tuesday afternoon Masses at Jesus House as well. Those Masses are always so special to me. It doesn't matter who the celebrant is, I always feel saturated in prayer and enfolded in God's love when I am there. Even though I now live a bit farther away, I still come back as often as I can.

I can't tell you how important it is for me to know that I can just show up at Jesus House whenever I want. The chapel is always there, always open, always ready for me. I sometimes go in just to sit and be quiet in the presence of the Blessed Sacrament. That's important to me. Angie always told me that it was because the Eucharist is there on the property that Jesus House remains through thick and thin. It is this presence that people feel when they first step foot onto the grounds.

It was the month of July when I made my Confirmation. Two people from Jesus House stood with me at the ceremony. Immediately after that, I attended a ten day silent, contemplative retreat at Jesus House. The timing was perfect! In fact, I can see that it all needed to happen that way. During this retreat, the retreatants must stay on the grounds the entire time. There is no radio, no TV, no internet. This became a very precious time for me. I was connecting. I was getting to know this God of ours – so loving, so merciful. Of course, every now and then I found myself meditating more on food, "Hmmm, I wonder what we are having for lunch?" The food was so delicious! Every now and then I even guessed right.

The people who made that retreat turned out to be some of the most inspirational people I have ever met. Many had been coming for years. To me, it was like entering in to the Communion of Saints for the very first time. They were beautiful souls. Some were in their eighties, some had a bit of difficulty getting around. Just to sit in the room with them was a spiritual experience for me.

Each day of the retreat I would go outside to the beautiful grounds, roses blooming in the garden nearby, and I would make the Stations of the Cross, following the little markers encircling the Chapel. Every day this walking prayer had a different impact on me. I had never been exposed to the Way of the Cross before I became Catholic. Somewhere in the process of faithfully walking around to each station, I discovered that it was like following the stations of my own life.

Sooner or later we are all forced to give up our own particular version of things, our preferences, and so we are led to a place we do not necessarily wish to go. Sooner or later we must learn to surrender ourselves and be willing to fall down, to struggle and to receive help from someone else. Each station has an exquisite lesson, or layer of lessons, which unfolded before me. There have been times when strangers helped me and times when I comforted them. There were times when everything was taken away and I was left feeling exposed, and times when my body, such as it is, had to die. But then – Easter! We are Easter people, after all! We are raised up and given new life and a new body – right here, right now. And when we truly encounter Christ, we are lighter, no longer weighed down by all our stuff and so we are able to serve. Some days during the retreat I would start at a different station - maybe the fifth, or the seventh – and I'd go around. Like life itself, it goes along just as it should.

On the last day of the retreat, it happened to be my birthday. I say happened, but I don't believe that it just happened that way. God had it in mind for me. I know that now. From the beginning of time, He had planned for me to be here, at this time, on this special day, at Jesus House. Yes, it was indeed, my "birth" day!

Quite some time later I attended the "Welcoming Prayer" weekend retreat at Jesus House. I learned that, in this type of prayer, the soul willingly gives up its own desires – the desire for security, the desire for affection and the overpowering desire for control. The process of learning to detach from unnecessary things was like sanding a piece of driftwood. The more we sanded, the more we could shine! It sounds easy but it was difficult. Finally, however, I was able to say, "Dear Lord, I give up the desire to change what I am experiencing in my life. I accept the pain, the struggles, the uncertainty. Let it be, dear Lord, let it be."

Along this path with Jesus House I began to discover that God was indeed orchestrating all these things in my life. I discovered it. But I had not yet embraced it. That came during a book study which was led by Angie. The book was Jean-Pierre de Caussade's "Abandonment to Divine Providence." It was during this time that I was finally able to accept and to embrace as truth, the fact that God was in control of my life...He always was, but I never saw it before. I never saw it before I came to Jesus House. I live in gratitude for the grace and the gifts given to me at Jesus House.

… … … … … … … … … … … … … … … …

"I have heard it said that there is no time with God
– that everything is present to Him.
That's what it's like with those
we grew to know and love at Jesus House.
Everything is "present,"
everything is "gift,"
and everything is "presence."'
Clare

… … … … … … … … … … … … … … … … … … … …

A New Man

"For through the law I died to the law,
that I might live for God.
I have been crucified with Christ;
yet I live, no longer I, but Christ lives in me."
(Galatians 2:19 - 20)

Hank

My story begins at the time of my divorce. After thirty three years, my marriage was ending. I needed help. I needed to find God in all this. Without knowing where to turn, I started coming to the Tuesday Masses at Jesus House. Thank God that I did. There I met a group of loving, accepting people who listened to me, comforted me and who, most importantly, prayed for me.

Not long afterwards I heard that the prayer group at Jesus House had been invited to run a "Life in the Spirit' seminar at the Church of Saint Mary of the Assumption in Hockessin. By that time I had made many truly good friends at Jesus House, all of whom seemed to be a part of the Charismatic movement. Since I had only a rough idea of what that actually meant, I decided that I would attend the seminar. It lasted six weeks.

By the end of that time, I knew for certain that Jesus was with me, that He had never left me and that He had been right by my side, all through the difficult times. I knew that He would always be there and that I never was, nor ever would be, alone. Up until that time, I had professed belief in this, but deep down inside of me, I doubted it. I believe that this is because I never took the time, nor had the courage, to really allow myself to live in and through this light.

Over the years I have become a part of the Healing Team at Jesus House. I have given talks and presentations at days of renewal and I have volunteered to help during retreats and fundraisers. To say that I wanted to share my new found joy and happiness and zeal is an understatement. I became a Eucharistic Minister for my parish, bringing the Blessed Sacrament to the homebound and hospitalized. It was the perfect way for me to share my faith and to do for others what the loving and generous people at Jesus House had done for me.

For the last several years, my health has been poor to say the least. Yet, through it all, the deep joy and knowledge that I am loved, and not alone, keeps me moving ever forward. It is because I constantly, or perhaps perennially, experience the love of God through the hands of His people – especially those at Jesus House. All my anger and fear has been turned to love and expectant faith. Truly, I can say I am a new man.

Now, not a night goes by that I do not pray for everyone - and I mean everyone - the Lord brings to my mind before I go to sleep.

Sometimes I will pray for as many as forty or fifty people in one night. It calms me down to do this and helps me to fall asleep. It brings much needed peace into my life, which can often be painful because of my on-going health issues. I wouldn't trade my time at Jesus House for anything in the world. It, quite literally, saved my life.

....

"They all ate and were satisfied."
(Matthew 14:20)

<u>Chris</u>

I remember once when Monsignor Sheers called me and asked if Jesus House would be able to take in a family of migrant workers - husband wife, son and daughter-in-law and 9 kids. I was not happy about it because I had just worked really hard to clean the whole place from top to bottom and I wanted it to stay clean since a big group was scheduled to come in for a retreat. It made good sense to say no. I wanted to say no. But I just couldn't. So I told the Monsignor that I would call him back.

As I was sitting there, going back and forth over the pros and cons, trying to convince myself that Jesus would say yes, our kids came into the room. "We have to help them," they said. "We have to say yes." I told Angie. Within the hour, the family arrived. In they came – the family and all their kids. We had only one pound of pasta in the house which Angie quickly cooked up. We served the pasta with milk and bread. Miraculously, on that little bit of food, every one ate until they were full and quite content, and there was plenty left over. Impossible! But there it was, right before my eyes.

The family stayed for several days. They messed up the entire place as any busy family would do, but the women of the family always cleaned up right way and kept the whole place sparkling clean. The young boys of the family worked on our cars, in appreciation for the help we were giving them. In the end, they left Jesus House in much better shape than they had found it.

And so I learned that even with all the "business" of Jesus House which had to be handled, day in and day out, the Lord was still asking us to say yes. To this day, I use this as the guideline for my life.

....

Father Tom Hanley, who became the Spiritual Director for Jesus House came one day with a man named Bill Dougherty who was a writer for the old Bulletin newspaper. When the paper went under he was out on his own with no job. Father Hanley assured everyone that Bill needed only some temporary housing and would be with stay at Jesus House only a few days. But Bill was suffering terribly after the blow of being laid off and was not prepared for the new electronic communications which were making their way into the history of the world. He ended up living at Jesus House for 10 years. When retreats took place he would go to live with a friend or at another retreat house. When he got sick, Chris would drive him to the VA because he had been in the marines. At one time there seemed to be a problem with proof of his citizenship because the government assumed he was born in Canada. But, with Chris' help, everything was put in order and Bill was awarded his full social security benefits. And, when they computed the benefits which had previously been denied to him, Bill walked away with a check totaling about $18,000.00. Bill finally had a nest egg and some income so that he could go back out on his own. At his funeral, the friends he made a Jesus House recalled how each of them had, at some time, driven Bill somewhere.

....

A Heart of Flesh

"A new heart I will give you,
and a new spirit I will put within you;
and I will take out of your flesh the heart of stone
and give you a heart of flesh."
(Ezekiel 36:26)

<u>Ginger</u>

I am an old timer – one of the originals. I've been here since we had to use the small dining room in the big house for our chapel. Most of all I recall how very beautiful the music was during our prayer meetings and at our Masses. It always seemed to touch my heart so deeply. We would sing, "Lord prepare me to be a sanctuary," and I knew that's what I wanted: to be a sanctuary for the Lord – a resting place. Every time I came to attend a meeting or to pray at Mass or to volunteer in some way or another, I would receive a healing. I know that's hard to believe but it's true. Something deep inside of me changed or grew. I felt as if my heart became larger and larger. I could welcome in more and more people, more and more situations. And the more I allowed in, the more I had to give away. I can't explain it really except to say that my time at Jesus House proved to be, and continues to be, a great healing experience for me.

Because my background was in teaching, I found my niche by helping with the family retreats. I would work with the kids during the breakout sessions. We'd sing songs and re-enact Bible stories. We would dance and twirl and clap. It was so much fun!

Beautiful friendships emerged and lasted. It was at Jesus House that I met a woman who offered a teaching job to me with her computer technology company. I took it and ended up working there for several years. We continue to be the best of friends. Those were the kind of relationships that were forged at Jesus House. The more I gave, the more I received. What a lesson on spiritual economics. The more I opened my heart, the more it was filled with joy! It is a blessed and sacred place.

Tom

It was during a Cursillo retreat at Jesus House that the needs of Jesus House caught my attention. Somehow I knew that this is where the Lord wanted me to serve. I knew that I needed to step down from a few of my volunteer activities at my parish, but until I stepped on to the grounds at Jesus House that weekend, I could not imagine what else He wanted me to do. I began to help Angie and Chris with bill paying and records keeping until the time came that they could afford an accountant. I was blessed to be there as the new Chapel was being built and, as a little bonus, I was able to have the old altar from the small chapel donated to my mother's nursing home at the Franciscan Health Care Center. It was dedicated to "Grand-mom Eleanor Burns" - my mom.

I was blessed as well to help start one of our most successful fundraisers: the Annual Golf Tournament. Ciro Poppiti did all the legal work for free and continues to serve on the Board of Directors as our legal advisor. Father Thomas Hanley, who was with us from the very beginning, is still our spiritual advisor even though he officially retired and now lives quite a distance away.

It was incredible to watch the Lord take our meager efforts and multiply them. We welcomed close to 100 golfers and sponsors! This annual event continues even today and is a vital part of the funding which Jesus House uses to support several outreach projects.

Jane

In all honesty, I can tell you that Jesus House has helped me grow spiritually more than any other place. And it is equally honest to tell you that Jesus House itself is a true work of the Holy Spirit, using Chris and Angie as His tools. When you listen to the stories of others who have come and gone through Jesus House, you will discover that it is impossible to deny that the Holy Spirit has been directing the whole project from the very beginning.

In the early days, I loved spending time in the chapel, which was in the old house. A friend and I would sit on the lumpy couch and share our faith walks, and pray with Jesus. How I cherish these memories! The days of renewal I attended, the book discussions, the retreats and time spent just working in the garden – all of these memories are precious to me. Now, though I live far away, these memories sustain me in times of difficulty or suffering.

Later on, when I became a spiritual director, I was privileged to work at Jesus House as a staff member. It was truly one of the happiest times of my life - working in that chilly, damp office, tucked away in the basement of the chapel; trying to convince the computer to do what we wanted, hoping the copy paper didn't curl in the dampness, keeping warm when the snow reached the two foot mark. And always there were friends who would make their way down the creaky wooden staircase just to stop by and say hello. It was a gift to have been able to work at a place that I loved – really loved. What a blessing to have worked side by side with two people who did what most of us only talk about - turning our lives over to the Lord completely! Nothing except grandchildren in Texas could have dragged me away.

Angie remains an inspiration to me, as well as a dear friend. And Chris' bear hugs are epic! I can never thank them enough for their "yes" to the Lord, for listening to the Holy Spirit, and for taking so many risks to create such a warm, welcoming and totally wonderful place for people to come to deepen their faith, to ponder the mystery of God, and to listen for his voice. Though I watch from a distance now, the courage and strength of these two people continues to lift me up and keep me moving forward, day by day, on my journey - or perhaps I should say adventure – with the Lord!

… … … … … … … … … …

"I can tell you this:
The Holy Spirit is going down your street
here at Jesus House!"
Pastor Anthony

… … … … … … … … … … … … … … …..

Kevin

My wife and I met Chris and Angie almost a year before Jesus House came into being. Our kids were about the same age and we often cam, family style, to attend the prayer meetings held in their home. As the kids played upstairs, the adults would gather in the living room for fellowship, fun, sharing and, of course, prayer.

During that time Clare (my wife) and I had been writing and playing music for several of the local parishes in the area and for the prayer group. The music was received with enthusiastic support and we had been considering proposals for producing an album. The collection of music we had decided upon for this album was the result of countless hours of prayer, begging the Lord for discernment, and the courage and humility to do all of it for His glory alone. It was the music of the heart; it was the music of the soul and came from the depths of our prayers. We were not ready to simply hand it over to just anyone. We wanted to make sure that we would not be forced to alter or omit or add anything. After all, this was not our work, but the work of the Holy Spirit. So we waited, and we prayed.

I remember one night very clearly. It was early in the evening on a bitterly cold November day. The dark was coming on quickly and I was sitting in the little living room area of the big house gazing out at the barren, brittle trees and the stark, threatening sky. I was working within the archetype of corporate America at that time. Or perhaps I should say I was stuck there – imprisoned by my own fear. I had a family to support and bills to pay. Our family's medical bills were skyrocketing, the company was cutting costs and lay-offs were an everyday occurrence. Let me just say that I desperately needed the silence and peace of Jesus House.

From somewhere deep within me, words and a little melody seemed to bubble up.

"The Lord is coming; He's bringing joy, and hope. Prepare you heart."

It came from desolation and fear which, up until that point, I had successfully stuffed down inside of me. I argued with Jesus.

"I don't have the gifts I need to sing out. I don't have equipment. I don't know where to start and even if I did I don't have the courage to do it."

My thoughts went on and on.

In a sort of reply the words and music continued.

"Hold on tight, my friend. It's time to fly; the moment is right. Don't ask me why. Just place your trust in me and take my hand. I died for You! Hold on tight, my friend. Leave all your fears behind. It's time to fly. Believe and take my hand."

Later on I shared the experience the melody and the lyrics with my wife. We decided to name the song "Christy's Song," after her aunt who was a nun.

It was at this time that Chris made that landfall commission on his job which ultimately resulted in the emergence of Jesus House. One night, when the prayer meeting in his home was over, Chris called me aside. We took a few steps away from the rest of the prayer group who were already laughing and chatting or calling up towards the second floor to retrieve their equally chatty children.

"Kevin," he said, smiling gently, "Angie and I have prayed about this and we want to give you $5,000.00 – no strings attached – so that you can produce your album on your own."

I was speechless. That much money in the 60's was – well, you do the math!

When I told Clare, we both cried. We were so grateful. In 1975, the album, "All the Roads," was produced and hit the market. It was the best of our best music up to that time. Hearts were touched and sales took off reaching even the international market. We were on our way. None of this would have happened if Chris and Angie had not received the grace and courage to trust God and to give everything to him with no thought of return.

The song, "Priceless in His Eyes," from the album remains one of Chris' favorites. To this day, every now and then he will ask us to play that particular song at the prayer meetings that continue, once a week, even after all these years.

Clare

Our son had been born with a heart condition. We were so worried, so unprepared to deal with something like this. If it had not been for the overwhelming compassion and prayers from people, especially those we met at Jesus House, I don't know how we would have survived. They put the word out for prayer throughout the Charismatic community. The whole East Coast was praying for us.

When the scheduled five hour surgery went into overtime – six hours, seven, ten, eleven hours – knowing that so many people were praying for us kept our faith and hope alive. We knew we were being carried through the ordeal. We could feel it. My son was only five years old and this was his third surgery. Afterwards, when we were permitted to see him - covered in gauze with so many tubes and surrounded by so many machines and blinking lights, we were tempted to panic all over again. But then my husband took his hand, put his face up close to my son's ear and whispered, "Can you hear me, son?" After only a few seconds he squeezed my husband's thumb. He heard. He knew that we were there with him. He was going to be okay. And so were we.

Today he is in his forties and while his health will always be precarious, he is doing fine! By the grace of God, we all made it through the storm.

There are so many wonderful and heart-warming memories which come to mind. Once during a prayer meeting, all the kids were on the second floor of the big house playing together as we prayed, one floor beneath them. Suddenly there was a big crash, lots of shrieks which turned immediately into shrieks of laughter and giggles. We never missed a beat.

"Oh Lord," someone prayed out loud, "We thank you that no one was killed up there just now."

But some of my fondest memories of Jesus House revolve around the wonderful meals we often shared. Families would get together every now and then. Everyone would bring something and we would all pile into the big house with our crock pots and casseroles. The friendships that developed have passed the test of time. We shared about everything – not just religion. Today these associations remain intact. We can come and go and be away for years at a time and still pick up right where we left off when we reconnect. I have heard it said that there is no time with God – that all things are present to him. That's what it's like with those we grew to know and love at Jesus House. Everything is "present," everything is "gift," and everything is "presence."

We still come and sing at the Healing Masses once a month. I pray we always will.

.

… … … … … … … … … ….

…………………………………………

Forty years of faithfulness, forty years of walking across deserts
and through raging waters,
forty years of seeing and serving Jesus in one another
as we move towards the Promised Land.
Jesus House has a future
and only God knows what it is.

Frank

…………………………………………

Available and Expectant

"The woman ... said to the people,
'Come see a man who told me everything I have done.
Could he possibly be the Messiah?'"
(John 4: 28-29)

132

<u>Sylvia</u>

Every October I bring my senior's group from Saint Mary's Church to Jesus House. We are called 'The Sages.' Once a year we plan our retreat. One of the priests from the diocese always officiates and of course, he says Mass for us. Over the years, Jesus House has become sort of a home away from home for the Sages. It is a familiar and welcoming place. When we arrive (always very early) for the scheduled program, we know that we will be greeted by the aroma of fresh coffee and good things to eat. It's a place where we know we will be well-fed spiritually too. The Chapel, always open, always available, seems to be waiting for us to come in and pray. Available, open and expectant – I guess you could say that this is how our souls should be as well.

> *"Amen, I say to you, unless you turn*
> *and become like children,*
> *you will not enter the kingdom of heaven."*
> *(Matthew 18:3)*

It is natural for me to want to give back. I come and work in the kitchen when Jesus House hosts retreats. I just love to see the kids come and go and to hear their appreciative groans as they reach for meatball sandwiches, or French fries or chocolate cake. This keeps me young in mind and heart and spirit. It reminds me to be joyful and grateful. And I enjoy cleaning up after them. In fact, I love it.

It's also really important to me to be able to see and know people like Angie and Chris who have, quite literally, given up everything

– money, security, time, property and possessions – for the Lord. I see the way the Lord gives back to them, supports them, and sends whatever they need at the time they need it. Seeing their example makes me more courageous in my efforts to give back – not as courageous as they are, but without their example I might be too afraid, too timid, too cautious to put myself out there with no visible means of return. I thank God for that most of all.

……………………….

"When the centurion who stood facing him
saw how he breathed his last he said,
"Truly this man was the Son of God!"
(Mark 15:39)

Jim

I was the Captain of Police for Wilmington for many years. My wife, Delores, would come to help with the retreats for the seriously ill. Though I was busy, I helped when I could. A little nun from Philadelphia who had severe arthritis wanted to come to the meetings but the drive was very hard for her so I would pick her up. She looked like such a fragile little woman but she was a tough one. We'd listen to the ball games as we drove back and forth on the Blue Route. Sometimes her mother came as well.

Little by little, I got to know some of the people at Jesus House. I was especially impressed by the good Christian men I met there. I would accompany my wife for one thing or another, until finally, one day I remember thinking to myself, "Why doesn't God touch my life the way I see Him touch others?" I could see Him at work in the lives of other men, like Tom Burns and Butch Ciabattoni. Tom told me that He made pact with God, to give his life over to Him. That was what I saw in Tom and I wanted that. "But," I said to myself, "God has never touched me." Up until that point I had not recognized God's works in my life. It seems that God heard my simple complaint that day.

Not long afterwards, something just sort of lit up inside me. It was like a light had turned on somewhere deep within. I remember the day like it was yesterday. I was on the road, driving to take my boards for my graduate degree when it suddenly hit me. Something had to change! I stopped at a pay phone and called Delores to tell her that I had decided to retire, to take my pension. It was a real turning point in my life. I realized that all the really good things in my life had come from God – from his orchestration, his direction, his mitigation. It was a real revelation to me. I could see clearly that He had indeed touched me throughout my life. He helped me in sports, in my marriage and in my career and I realized that it was time for me to give back. I wanted to give back. That very day, quietly driving alone in my car, I gave my life to the Lord and I know it was because of what I had seen and heard and experienced at Jesus House that this happened. I can't tell you how good it has been to know that the people at Jesus House were praying for me and that they still pray for me. They always will.

… … … … … … … … … ….

"But he said to the woman,
"Your faith has saved you; go in peace."
(Luke 7: 50)

Edie

I had first come to Jesus House to be built up in my faith and it seemed that, through the many trials and challenges of Jesus House, He was answering my prayer. We worked continually on a zero-based budget and every day, just exactly what was needed came in. Every day, people called in for prayer. They had family problems, financial problems and health problems – very serious stuff. And every day, because of the strength we gained from our own trials and difficulties, we were able to pray for the callers with humble courage.

And this was just the periphery of the ministries which poured out of Jesus House. In the background, larger and larger groups began to call us to schedule retreats. With no staff to speak of except myself, it was Chris and Angie who made the beds and emptied the trash cans, welcomed visitors and served them coffee.

I became the part-time secretary, girl Friday, and chief cook and bottle washer. In the beginning, I was able to handle the day to day operational and secretarial needs and still oversee the management of our different building projects. It was a time that was wonderful but certainly not without its own challenges. As you can imagine, the pay was low since more often than not, we could barely make payroll. There were many evenings when my husband and I labored over our finances. But then, God, who must use such circumstances to strengthen our faith, would see to it that a check would come – just in time!

The director of the board once reminded us that the bumble bee should, technically speaking, be unable to fly. He always used this analogy when speaking of Jesus House which, technically, should have never been able to get off the ground, but was, all the same, flying free in the breath of the Holy Spirit. For sixteen wonderful years I worked there, three days a week. To this day, Jesus House holds some of my fondest memories.

....

"Jesus turned and saw them following him
and said to them...
'Come, and you will see.'
So they went and saw where he was staying,
and they stayed with him that day."
(John 1: 38 – 39)

Arlene

I first came to Jesus House for their community Bible study which Angie was teaching at the time. The year was 1992. I saw a tiny ad in our church bulletin for a community bible study. I had never been to a bible study before and I thought that this was something I needed. So off I went, Bible in hand!

First, I met Angie, then I learned about Jesus House, its vision, its mission and purpose. I heard about the retreats and conferences, and I learned that they had a prayer group. It all sounded very good to me. During that time, I had been experiencing a series of challenges with my daughter. Something was changing in her life and I did not know why or what to do about it. It seemed to me that the prayer group might be helpful though I had never been exposed to such a thing before. The group was charismatic. They were praying in tongues, and I had no idea what that was or what I was expected to do.

A man by the name of Joe Conte was there with his wife. He was a kind and wonderful man who took me under his wing, and explained the Charismatic Renewal to me. Joe was a deacon. His wonderful understanding of Scripture and Church ritual, coupled with his charismatic gifts of the Holy Spirit, made him the mentor I had been hoping to find and his friendship was a great support to me as I walked with my daughter during her time of need.

As time went on I became a regular fixture at Jesus House. I watched, almost spellbound, as more and more people just seemed to show up. No one knew one another, they all just came. I began to participate in the day retreats and conferences. New programs were always being planned. They began a once-a-month day of reflection which really took off.

Being connected to Jesus House started to change my life in so many ways. I decided to go back to school. My family and friends thought I was nuts, but my friends at Jesus House encouraged me to pursue this dream. Well, I did it! In the year 2000 I completed my college education. I can't tell you how elated I was.

Then, one night, I was coming out of the chapel just as Chris was coming in. He stopped dead in his tracks, looked at me and said, "When are you coming here?"

"What?" I said, having been caught off guard. "What are you talking about?"

I could not imagine what he was talking about.

Chris smiled at me and said, "Come and work downstairs."

I thought he was nuts. I'm sure he knew that by the look on my face but he just continued smiling and repeated himself. "Come and work downstairs." Then he disappeared into the Chapel and I was left standing on the steps outside in the cool night air. After that first time, anytime he would see me, he would ask me again.

Finally I showed up one day and walked slowly down the Chapel steps to the small offices below. I did not know what I was supposed to do. I was just there. Chris and I would talk about baseball and other things. Sometimes I would answer the phone or run little errands. Slowly but surely, as new programs were developed, I became busier.

The family retreat program started up again. It was amazing to see how that endeavor was so blessed. We now had the buildings so that families could stay for a week. We were able to provide meals now. Teens came to help. My son came and volunteered his time with both kids and adults. He taught activities, games and even square dancing! It became obvious to everyone involved that God's plan was to keep these family retreats going as more and more families came.

All of this was generated by word of mouth, and the numbers just kept growing. Sometimes when people drove by and saw the sign they would just come in. Most of the time when they came, they wanted to talk with someone. And, as always, the Lord sent just the right person along at just the right time. This same phenomenon continues to this day and is a cause for our constant gratitude and thanksgiving.

Jerry

In the late 1970's, long before the chapel was built, Chris asked me to help him with a project. The grounds had been unattended over the years and were filled with vines, briers and scrub trees. I know that Chris was often big on ideas but short on just exactly how to get the thing done. This time, his big idea was to make a pathway through the wooded area. Once the pathway was in Chris wanted to construct Stations of the Cross along the way. It was the kind of project that required the right equipment, sufficient manpower and money for materials, none of which immediately presented themselves. At that time I taught horticulture at Delcastle High School so I had access to both power and hand tools and, as it turned out, I had plenty of students who were happy to assist me in this unique project.

I remember first stepping into the woods behind the main house. I suddenly felt like Moses leading his people because, beyond that first step, there was no plan.

The work was hard. It was like walking through a jungle with vines hanging from the trees, obstructing the view. Little by little we cut a path through the scrub. We chopped down small trees, made little clearings, changed direction and started again. It was difficult to see any progress as we moved slowly along. But, over the period of a few weeks, though the power mower broke down and the kids drifted away to attend to their studies, the property was completely cleared! The first leg of Chris' big idea had been accomplished.

Dorothy

Somewhere around the year 1976-77 my husband and I attended the Catholic Charismatic Conference in Atlantic City, New Jersey. As we were driving back to our home in College Park, Maryland, we came across three people hitch-hiking along the highway. We stopped an asked where they were going. They said, "Jesus House" in Wilmington, Delaware. We had never heard of Jesus House but we told them to get in and we would take them there. They said that their car had broken down and they were stranded. They were very quiet and, I have to admit, we thought they were a little crazy. We kept eyeing them during the ride, wondering what we had gotten ourselves in to. We thought to ourselves, "These are strange folks."

When we came to Wilmington they gave us sketchy directions such as: just go up this road, okay now go left here." Finally we came up to a park-like setting and pulled up to a large house. Out front was a sign that read: "Jesus House." The door was open and the three invited us in for a few minutes. We did not stay long. We accepted their thanks and started to pull away. But before we left I asked their names. As it turns out, two of our mysterious passengers were Chris and Angie Malmgren. So it seems, looking back across all those years, that these strange people did know where they were going. And we had the rare and wonderful blessing of coming to Jesus House in the very beginning – we have been friends of Jesus House ever since.

....

"Jesus said, 'Let the children come to me,
and do not prevent them;
for the kingdom of heaven belongs to such as these.'"
(Matthew 19:14)

One day, a friend of Jesus House showed up bringing with her a woman who was in tears. Someone had dropped this woman off at an abortion clinic a few hours earlier. The woman spoke almost no English at all. She just kept crying, and saying, "My baby, my baby..." The volunteers from Jesus House who greeted her needed a translator so they called two young girls they knew who spoke Spanish. With their help, the woman regained her composure and was able to relay what was happening. She was from Peru. Her husband had been brought over by a local company to be a carpet layer. When she and her husband arrived in the United States they were told that it was against the law for an unregistered person to be pregnant because the child to be born would automatically become a U.S. citizen. They were being threatened with jail and deportation.

The Jesus House volunteers started calling local government officials and were finally able to speak with Senator Bill Roth who said that there was no such U.S. law and that she did not have to undergo an abortion. With that problem solved, the volunteers went to work getting medical help for the woman. It was discovered she had tuberculosis. Pregnant and suffering with tuberculosis! Now what was to be done? God, it seems, had a plan.

Senator Roth responded once again and engaged his staff to help. They found a place in Colorado which would treat her tuberculosis and would also help her to deliver her baby.

Many years later, early in 2014, a call came in to Jesus House from a woman named Hilda – the lady from Peru. She, and her husband Richard now live nearby and the baby, a girl, just graduated from college. Praise God!

"Do not neglect hospitality,
for through it some have unknowingly entertained angels."

(Hebrews 13:2)

<u>Angie</u>

A young man and his wife came here once, many years ago. Both were struggling to be free from dependence on drugs and to find their way in life. We prayed with them.

After some time they became members of a Christian ministry group which had originated in Texas. Both entered training for ministry and, in time, both were ordained. Many years later, they started the Victory Christian Fellowship Ministry located in Bear, Delaware. Every now and then we hear from them. They call just to keep in touch and to say thanks again for taking care of them during a time when they were down and out.

"And the king will say to them in reply,
'Amen, I say to you, whatever you did
for one of these least brothers of mine,
you did for me.'"
(Matthew 25: 40)

Then there was Gretchen Jackson, a graduate from Neumann University with a degree in pastoral counseling. She came for a visit to Jesus House one day and decided, as so many do, to stay connected, offering her services as a Pastoral Counselor. She and her husband owned a beautiful horse, Barbaretta who had won the Kentucky Derby. One day, she came to tell us that they had received some stock and, while this was a good thing, it would put them in a higher tax bracket which was not to their benefit. They wanted to donate the stock to Jesus House to provide for a camp for those suffering with AIDS. Now this took place during a time when AIDS was considered too contagious and far too dangerous to be dealt with by the general public.

Soon afterwards, religious Sister, by the name of Delores Mackland, convinced Angie and Chris to become involved in a project organizing junior high kids to collect toys, bikes, clothes and more for children with the disease. It was difficult for them since they had children of their own and were worried about the possibility of inadvertently spreading this disease to their own family. But after prayer and a good bit of soul searching, they agreed and the project took off. Under Chris's watchful eye, groups of junior high students collected and distributed Christmas gifts for children with AIDS.

One of the children was a beautiful 3 year old girl who born to a mom with AIDS. Everyone knew that the little girl would not live long. When Chris walked in the room with the teens carrying gifts, she hugged Chris and asked him if he was Santa Claus. Chris could not hold up under the sadness that overwhelmed him at her innocent and hopeful question. He went out to car and cried. Later he went to Sister Delores' office to tell her that he could no longer participate in this endeavor because he was simply too weak. Looking him straight in the eye and without the slightest hesitation Sister Delores said, "God said you can do it for Him!" Her words took Chris out of himself and allowed him to see his place in God's plan. "I had been doing this for me," he said. "I forgot that I am really doing this for Him!"

This beautiful but difficult ministry saw many such circumstances. The teens knew that many of the kids who were receiving these gifts would have very little time to use them. But this did not deter them. In fact, it had just the opposite effect. It energized and strengthened them, and filled them with the determination to get these gifts to these little ones.

The project resulted in a beautiful Trinitarian blessing: The sick children were blessed with a joyful Christmas and experience the love of Jesus through the teenagers who came to visit them. The teens themselves realized the value and gift of going beyond their comfort zones to bring the love of God to others, and Angie and Chris experienced, first hand, the providence and power of yet another "Yes!"

All Are Welcome

....

"Jesus House, to me, seems to be a temporary, pass-through
place of love and peace where we - weary travelers in life -
can find rest, and the reassurance
that there is a loving, caring God
who comes to us and helps us through other people.
Jesus House is that place.

I had to stay longer than most,
because I think I had the most struggles in my life,
and I was just plain slow when it came to "getting it."
I do not know what other road I would have traveled
if it were not for Jesus House.
There are two special places in my life
and I know I will never depart from either of them:
The Sacred Heart of Jesus, and Jesus House."
Drew

....

We heard from people of many different Christian denominations, though we were never really sure how they even heard of Jesus House. For example, a beautiful group of women from an African

American Christian Community in Dover showed up one year for a retreat. Year after year, they continued to come for meetings, retreats and prayer time.

Another time, we received a phone call from the board of directors of the Faith City Congregation here in Wilmington. They wanted to know if someone from Jesus House could come to them and facilitate a Life in the Spirit Seminar. The pastor said that he had heard that the Catholic Church was experiencing a renewal in the Holy Spirit and he wanted to know more about it. His teachers needed more of the Holy Spirit, he said.

Over the years we welcomed several memorable people to Jesus House. One year, a beautiful Baptist minister, Pastor Fern, came to Jesus House. She brought parishioners here for a retreat. Ron Snyder, author of "Christians in an Age of Hunger," came to Jesus House with his wife. Angie encouraged them to move to Delaware and they now live nearby.

...................…...

The Gates of Heaven

"I will give you the keys to the kingdom of heaven."
(Matthew 16: 19)

<u>Angie</u>

What a blessing it was to have Pastor Anthony knock on the door of Jesus House many years ago. She is the pastor of the Gates of Heaven Church in Wilmington and was looking for a place to hold her Sunday 5:00 pm services. Welcoming Pastor Anthony to Jesus House turned out to be a triple blessing to all involved. Jesus House hosts AA meetings every Sunday evenings at 7:00 p.m., so when Pastor Anthony's services started up, many of those attending the AA meetings would come early to attend her service before their meeting. She, in turn, would talk to some of the members about volunteering at Jesus House. She coached one particular member who still comes to help us serve meals when we host retreats. Than man is now a deacon for her Church. Pastor Anthony and Gates of Heaven Church continue to hold their Sunday evening prayer services here in our Chapel.

....

The originators of the Men's Weekend Ministries flew in to Jesus House from Ohio. Jack Wente, who was instrumental in getting this program up and running, would walk around the property hugging trees; He was so happy to have our beautiful grounds to walk on because he lived in the city where there was no opportunity for him to enjoy nature. He had a long beard, and was so happy and comfortable and appreciative of nature that for many of us, he became a Saint Francis of Assisi. Jack, however, was a truck driver with five grown sons. They were all "motorcycle guys."

Jack shared with us the story of the murder of one of his beloved sons. He was shot during a fight somewhere on the city streets of Cleveland. The killer was arrested, charged, tried for murder and found guilty. He and his sons found the courage to walk up to the man after the trial and to forgive him, one by one. They were able to let go of the tendency toward any grudge or need for revenge. Each one was grateful to have this stone removed from his heart. From that time on, every Good Friday, Joe walked the streets of Cleveland with a big Cross, praying the Stations of the Cross and handing out bibles. He was a great evangelist.

Chris

My dad came and lived here at Jesus House for a while. He was getting old and struggling with dementia. We had to put his pie in the blender so that he could eat it! Angie was so good about it; no one else could have put up with dad. Most members of my family could not be around him for too long without becoming overwhelmed by his needs.

But he caught the vision of Jesus House and he really wanted to help. Now, painting was dad's thing and he was good at it. I remember once purchasing some beautiful exterior house paint; it was a deep green. Later that day, when I was returning home from a meeting, I discovered that the driveway been painted green. Another day I returned home to find that all the outside porch furniture had been painted in driveway tar. "Boy," he huffed, wiping his brow and smiling at me, "That paint is tough!"

It was difficult watching him struggle. Before the dementia set in he was as smart as a whip. But then came a day when several men from the community were working on taking down some very old, overgrown trees. No one could get them down. My dad strolled over to the group, surveyed the situation and, putting his hand on my shoulder, pointed up to one of the tree tops. "Just tie a rope on that front branch," he said, squinting into the sun. "Then just pull it down in this direction." Two of the men managed to get the rope up to the top of the tree. My father then took the end of the rope and pulled hard. Without the slightest bit of trouble, the tree fell and landed exactly where he said it would land. With a big grin he looked at all us big, smart men standing around in a circle, scratching our heads. "You just have to look at it to know what to do," he said!

We often brought him to prayer group. Now my father was not a hugger. But when he would come to the prayer meetings and, before long, he began to hug and to show his emotions maybe for the first time in his life. The love and compassion he experienced there allowed him to step outside his comfort zone. Everyone else was hugging and dad simply joined in.

When he finally passed away, since he was not Catholic, we did not put the traditional Rosary beads in his hand. Instead we put a paint brush there.

. . . .

"For the Lamb ... will be their shepherd,
and he will guide them to springs of living water."
(Revelation 7:17)

One day, a man named Joe Duffy, and his wife Betty, who is now in her 90's, came to Jesus House. They loved it so much that Joe offered to bulldoze and grade the land while his wife cooked for retreats. Once the grading was completed, Joe decided to put in a water pump and made a startling discovery: An aquifer – a pristine underground spring that ran under the entire property! No one knew it was there. This discovery ended up saving Jesus House thousands upon thousands of dollars when the time came to provide water to the new buildings that eventually went up on the property. Tapping into the county water system for them would have been almost impossible.   This is why Jesus House now has the most crystal clear, best tasting spring water in Delaware! For these forty years, the water has been plentiful, services all the facilities on the grounds.

Joe and his wife were devout Catholics. They loved the sacred Scriptures and felt so honored and happy to be a part of the many outreach ministries offered at Jesus House.   As time went on and Joe could no longer get around as easily as he once did, they attended a romantic weekend retreat held at Jesus House and sponsored by their parish. Everyone remembers when Betty would wink at her husband and call him "My Joe!"

The Best Kept Secret in Delaware

"Foxes have dens and birds of the sky have nests,
but the Son of Man has nowhere to rest his head."
(Matthew 8:20)

Pastor Anthony

My congregation had a small church at 3rd and Franklin in Wilmington, where I hosted 12 step meetings and ministered to whoever walked through the doors. One day a poor, dear girl, hooked on drugs came into my church. She said that she had heard of a place called Jesus House and that she wanted to go there. I had no idea where it was but agreed to find it and to bring her there. She had heard that there were prayer meetings held there every Tuesday night and she knew she needed prayer. She was desperate. I could tell she was on the brink of complete despair.

When we pulled up to Jesus House, I remember thinking that this was one of the most beautiful places I had ever seen, but it was the surprising feeling of peace which first really caught me off guard. It seems like the minute I stepped on to the property a grace just washed over me. I remember thinking to myself, "What's going on here?

We walked into the chapel as the prayer meeting started. We were met by silent smiles that were so warm and welcoming that no words were necessary, nor would have been sufficient to translate the loving embrace which we both experienced. Everyone there prayed for her. One by one they poured out their love and begged Jesus for His help. The more the love poured out, the more her tears poured out. It was like a great floodgate had been opened up from heaven. I was overwhelmed! I had always heard, and truly believed that prayer changes things, but this was the first time I actually saw it in action.

Over the next few years, if I found myself in the area I would stop in during the day to sit and pray by myself in the Chapel, or on a bench outside by the Stations of the Cross. After all, who ever heard of a chapel kept wide open day and night, every day of the year! I still can't get over that!

In the meantime, the people from the streets – the drug addicts, the homeless, the handicapped - continued to wander in to my little church in the city. Then one very sad day, I learned that the building, this place which my congregation had called home, was being condemned. Soon we would be homeless. I thought of Jesus and shrugged my shoulders. If He had been thrown out of the temple, why should I expect anything different? If he said, "The Son of Man has no place to lay his head," then why should this little flock complain? In the middle of these thoughts, I remembered Jesus House. "No, too far out of the way," I said to myself.

156

For the next several months I focused on helping those that came in from the streets to find places that could take them in. I drove them to rehab and helped them search out other resources. Every day I searched and searched for another place in the city, but there was "no room in the inn."

Then another addict showed up who wanted me to take them to the prayer meeting at Jesus House. By this time, I was so enmeshed in trying to find a place in the city that I had all but forgotten about Jesus House. I hadn't been there for months. It seemed like ages since I had been able to get back there. But when we showed up, the group remembered me and invited me to come back for the prayer meetings any time. And I did. I became acquainted with everyone, but I especially remember Issy.

"You and I have something in common," she told me one evening when the prayer meeting ended.

I smiled. "What's that?" I asked, taking her hand.

"My middle name is the same as your first name - Mercedes!"

After attending several meetings I mentioned my predicament to the prayer group to ask them for prayer. As we prayed, the scripture, "Ask and you shall receive" kept coming to me.

I held my breath and, not at all sure how everyone would respond, I asked if they might allow my little congregation to meet at Jesus House every Sunday evening. I remember that I felt honored at having the privilege to ask for such a favor. I was welcomed with open arms. But my heart was already beating loudly in my ears, so that the first thing I can really remember about that moment was the sight of Angie smiling at me as she told me, "We would be delighted to have you here at Jesus House for your Church meetings!" She hugged me tightly. One by one, everyone else did the same. "Greater love than this," I remember thinking, "no man has! And so began my long and beautiful relationship with Jesus House. It remains as vibrant and active today as it was so many years ago.

At one time there were twelve people from my ministry who wanted to be baptized, but I needed a pool, because we are Baptist and we liked to immerse the person in water for baptism. This was before it became so popular in the Catholic Church. Sure enough, I was told that there was a stream on the property! That was that! We set the date for the baptism.

The water that day was as clear and clean as the sunny sky which hovered over us all like the Holy Spirit himself. It was a Sunday afternoon. We all met at the big house. Those who were being baptized where dressed in white, while families and friends were in their Sunday finest! We formed a little procession and sang hymns as we walked across the beautiful property and made our way down to the creek. With the flowers peeking out from the woods around us it seemed to me as if all of creation was celebrating. After the Baptism we had a nice luncheon at the big house.

For years now, my little congregation meets every Sunday night in the Chapel at Jesus House. It's the Chapel of Saint Joseph the Worker. What could be more perfect? We meet right around the time the AA meeting takes place. I cannot count all the beautiful friendships and associations that have developed as a result. To this day a person or two will come in from their meeting and pray with us. Sometimes they ask for prayer.

I still come to the Tuesday night prayer meetings whenever I can, often bringing with me people from the inner city, sometimes just whoever happened to meet me on the street. When they move away, they still keep in touch. One man moved to Arkansas but still calls in for prayers now and then. It is exciting to see how the Lord works. They always say the same thing. They can feel the Holy Spirit at Jesus House.

There was a young man who used to live across the street from Jesus House. One day he just wandered in to see if he could help. Issy told him about my Sunday night services, and he soon became a regular attendee. I would meet him here at Jesus House so that we could speak about prayer, about Life in the Spirit and about ways to serve the Lord by serving one another. He was eager to learn God's ways.

I felt that the Lord wanted him to become a deacon, so I invited 7 experienced deacons - one of them Catholic - to help him and to pray for him. This young man became what my church calls a

159

"Walking Deacon." That is, one who serves while he is learning. He worked while he went to school to study. He was such a help to me in my ministry! He has since left this area because of his work, but he joined a new church and continues to work for the Lord in his new home.

One very particular thing I notice about those who come to Jesus House is that they are all able to work together. I have helped at the Catholic retreats and the people from Jesus House come and help me with mine. Everyone gets out of themselves and things get done. We all love the same God. My dad was a deacon in the Baptist Church. When I come here, I meet the deacons and priests, and the Eucharistic Ministers from the Catholic Church. It all fits together perfectly. My granddaughter said she loves Father John Hynes (one of the Catholic priests who worked with us at Jesus House) with her whole heart. Isn't that beautiful? When people ask me how I could work with so many Catholics, I always give them the same answer: "Because the common denominator is the Father, Son and Holy Spirit! We all worship the same God. In everything, He orders our steps!"

My health is not as good now as it used to be, but I keep pushing forward. Heaven is my goal, but I can tell you this: The Holy Spirit is going down your street here at Jesus House!

We call Jesus House "The best kept secret in Delaware!" And so it is. Hidden, like the Lord.

<u>Angie</u>

Recently, a lovely woman, seventeen years sober, came to Jesus House for prayer. She had just been diagnosed with advanced breast cancer and was struggling with God's presence in this situation. After attending our Tuesday afternoon mass, a group of those present prayed with her. She tearfully thanked them and left. When she went for her second set of tests the doctors discovered that her cancer was not aggressive. She went for her mastectomy and was at peace.

Then, one day when she was driving to Pittsburgh to join a reunion with her original AA group, her car was struck by a drunk driver. The accident resulted in the loss of part of her arm. Angie and Chris again went to be with her in the hospital. As she recovered she found herself in the unique position of helping those in the rehab hospital with her. Still in recovery from the accident she stays in touch with Jesus House, coming to the Days of Hope retreats and dinners. She remains filled with hope and joy - and with the peace which surpasses all human understanding.

Some stayed at Jesus House longer than others. Over time, so many have come and gone. Perhaps we will only know the whole of it when we get to Heaven. But it is safe to say that Jesus House is not a place to stay long, it is a place that makes it possible to respond to Jesus' word, "Come apart and rest awhile." Those who work and volunteer and pray for Jesus House have caught that vision and they keep it going. They work to make Jesus House a sacred space for weary travelers on the road to eternity.

....

When a new parish – Parish of the Resurrection – began to form in our neighborhood without a building or class rooms, Jesus House welcomed their parishioners and their children for CCD, day camps and RCIA. To this day, the parishioners remain grateful to Jesus House and support them in prayer, with works of mercy and financial donations.

....

"This poor widow put in more
than all the other contributors to the treasury."
(Mark 12:43)

Eleanor

"I remember when Jesus House moved in during the mid1970's. The property backs up to mine. "New neighbors," I thought to myself. So I brought over a cake to welcome the family to the neighborhood. I had heard what they had done and how they had given all their money to start a retreat center. The thought of it really baffled me. Imagine! Turning your whole life over to the providence of God! How does one do that and still live in the world? I had certainly heard of people doing that but I was having trouble believing that such a thing was possible. I have to admit, a big part of me was just curious to see these people and how they lived.

Although I liked what was going on at Jesus House and was impressed with the honesty and sincerity of everyone I met there, I didn't start to volunteer until my kids grew up. It was God's perfect timing, both for Jesus House and for me. I had no real religious education and the time I could give was very limited so I wasn't sure if I would be much help. But somehow I fit in. Of course back then there were not as many retreats as we have now. Over the years I have been with Jesus House, I have watched as it evolved from just a few retreats to a very busy retreat center.

I'm a quiet person and I don't really discuss religion very much, but I can't deny that I feel the Holy Spirit when I am here. Jesus House provided for me a simple yet substantial way to give something back to the Lord for all He has given me. Maybe a part of me just wanted to see if God would really honor such a thing. Needless to say, He has! And I've been coming to Jesus House ever since.

....

Best Friends Forever

<u>Spring</u>

I find Jesus House to be place that is both coated and infused with prayer. You feel it when you are here, especially when you step into the chapel. So many people have said the same thing. There are no coincidences with God.

One of the fondest memories I have of my earliest association with Jesus House revolves around a retreat I attended which focused on prayer, particularly centering prayer. I had been struggling with depression and knew I needed something to help me get and keep a peaceful balance in my life. When I saw the notice for this retreat, I thought that perhaps this type of prayer might be helpful. I had an idea of what Centering Prayer was, but had no real understanding of the process or the expected results.

As I worked through the retreat, meditating on the beautiful Scriptures which were given to us, I discovered that the word "joy" often caught my attention. I had been asking God to give me a sort of key-note for my life – a word, a thought, a concept that would be special to me, and sacred. In short I was asking Him for my own, personal sacred word. It was during this retreat that I believe I received it: joy! That was the deep longing of my heart. It was joy that I had been seeking – joy that I had been hoping for – but I just never called it by its true name. Now, I knew it.

164

Well, it must have been the right word because all that weekend I felt flooded with a great joy. I even danced around in my room at times and danced (as discreetly as I could) on the way to the chapel. I felt like a little kid whose body just had to express what was going on inside.

This joy, I soon discovered, brought with it the unexpected feeling of great, enfolding peace – it was a pervading peace that took root firmly in my heart. Both joy and peace remain with me now – my two constant friends, my companions on my journey of faith. If I ever lose sight of them, I stop what I am doing and look for them and do not continue on my journey unless we can all walk together, arm-in-arm – Best Friends Forever.

....

Angie

If we can hold the picture in our hearts that we are all brothers and sisters, then we all come through here and go off wherever the Lord sends us. But we always seem to come back to Jesus House because this place is where we have our roots. It is a loving, welcoming environment where one can come and be immersed in God's love. And when we leave, we take away with us whatever is needed. No one who has come to Jesus House is the same when they leave.

About the Author

Lynne Keating lives in Newark, Delaware, just a mile from Jesus House. It was at Jesus House that she was able to discern a life-changing move and to Jesus House that she returned years later, just as plans for marking its 40th Anniversary were being discussed. She spent the next year sitting down to chat with person after person who has passed through Jesus House over the last 40 years, to hear their stories first hand. The result is this book.

She tells us:

Life with the Lord is always an adventure – a fact that becomes very evident in these pages. This is not hear-say, or legend clouded by the passage of time, but the accounts of the people whose lives were, and continue to be, profoundly changed through their connection with one very special place.

Their stories confirm something I've been observing for more than a decade now. I see a strong and beautiful pattern developing today, especially apparent against the backdrop of upheaval and uncertainty. Story after story makes its way into the media describing remarkable acts of selfless love and a courageous willingness to lay down one's life for another. I am glad to be in the mix. After all, the adventure, I have discovered, has only just begun.

43596548R00097